THE ONE

CW00347396

Also by Richard Harries:

Seasons of the Spirit (USA: The Time of the Spirit),
ed., with G. Every and K. Ware (SPCK 1984)
Prayers of Hope (1975)
Turning to Prayer (1978)
Prayers of Grief and Glory (1979)
Being a Christian (USA: What Christians Believe) (1981)
Should a Christian Support Guerrillas? (1981)
Praying Round the Clock (1983)
The Authority of Divine Love (1983)
Prayer and the Pursuit of Happiness (1985)
Morning Has Broken (1985)
Christianity and War in a Nuclear Age (1986)
C. S. Lewis: The Man and his God (1987)

THE ONE GENIUS

—

READINGS THROUGH THE YEAR WITH AUSTIN FARRER

SELECTED BY RICHARD HARRIES

Foreword by Michael Ramsey

First published in Great Britain 1987
SPCK
Holy Trinity Church
Marylebone Road
London NW1 4DU

Introduction and this selection copyright © Richard Harries 1987

All rights reserved. No part of this book may
be reproduced or transmitted in any form or by any means,
electronic or mechanical, including photocopying, recording, or by any
information storage and retrieval system, without permission
in writing from the publisher.

British Library Cataloguing in Publication Data

Farrer, Austin
    The one genius: readings through the year
    with Austin Farrer.
    1. Devotional calendars
    I. Title   II. Harries, Richard *1936-*
    242'.2   BV4810

    ISBN 0-281-04269-1

        Printed in Great Britain
    at the University Printing House, Oxford

FOR DEREK

FOREWORD

Austin Farrer and I were contemporaries, and we met for the first time when we went as students to the Theological College at Cuddesdon. We walked together up the hill from Wheatley Station to the College and at once became friends. Like other friends of Austin, I sometimes felt a remark of his to be too profound to grasp, and a little later I laughed to think how gloriously simple it had really been. He was always one to whom the deep and the simple were of one piece.

Austin's father was a Baptist minister, and he was devoted to his parents. He became an Anglican during his time as an Oxford undergraduate, and remained one with a Tractarian style of deep and disciplined piety. After a curacy in Dewsbury, where he was very happy, he returned to Oxford and there remained for the rest of his life, being in succession Chaplain of St Edmund Hall, Chaplain and Fellow of Trinity College, and Warden of Keble. He and his wife Katharine were greatly loved for their friendship and hospitality, and Austin loved talking with young people whether on some profound subject or just talking for the fun of talking. He was through the Oxford years a theologian, teacher, poet and pastor, and for him theology and prayer were of one piece. He died suddenly two days after Christmas 1968.

Farrer's writings were numerous and varied, including profound works on philosophy, discussions of biblical interpretation, and simple expositions of Christian belief and worship. A theme common to them all was his conviction that God reveals himself through poetic images, and this conviction was developed in his Bampton Lectures with the characteristic title of *The Glass of Vision*.

Many will be grateful to the Dean of King's College London for his labour of love in compiling this anthology, and in reading it they will find the mind stirred and the heart refreshed, for the well is deep.

✠ Michael Ramsey
Durham 1986

INTRODUCTION

When C. S. Lewis's wife, Joy Davidman, died, the priest who took the funeral service was barely able to get the words out through his own tears. That priest, who ministered to both Lewis and his wife in their last years, was Austin Farrer. For Farrer was one of the very few modern Christian thinkers whom Lewis admired. When Farrer's book *Saving Belief* was published Lewis wrote:

> We have been deluged with theologies in which the most flamboyant pretensions to novelty and daring co-exist with the greatest thinness and flatness of content; Dr Farrer, remaining patient, modest and orthodox, opens new horizons to us on every other page.

Austin Farrer, who died in 1968 at the age of 62, spent nearly all his life teaching theology in Oxford where, in his last years, he was Warden of Keble College. Outwardly his life was uneventful enough. Yet he was sometimes called a genius. Indeed it has been said of him that he is the one genius that the Church of England has produced during this century.

What was the nature of Farrer's genius? Normally we use the word to indicate some overwhelming talent that a person possesses in the light of which all their personal qualities, good and ill, pale into insignificance. We talk about the genius of Shakespeare's drama, or Mozart's music or Giotto's paintings. In such cases it does not affect our opinion of their genius if we discover that they were emotionally childish, their political opinions obnoxious or their private life a mess. Farrer's genius was not of that kind. It consisted not of one talent but of three; three fused together in such a way that each reached its perfection in relation to the other two.

First, there was the sheer brilliance of Farrer's intellect. He obtained an outstanding first in Greats and after a short period in parish life returned to Oxford with a fellowship. He never lost the facility of turning a difficult English expression into idiomatic Latin or Greek. But people's minds are good in different ways. Some are quick and some are learned. Farrer was both learned and quick but his most important intellectual characteristic was the ability to think with clarity and perseverance about the most difficult questions in philosophy and theology. All his mental acuteness and wide reading were put at the service of worrying away at the most intractable problems. His wife recorded his method of working. He would sit down totally absorbed in thought for an hour or so then jump up with the words 'I think I'll write that one down'.

The second quality possessed by Farrer was the imagination of a poet. He was not himself a good poet, though he did write some verse. Instead he wrote some superb prose. He put all his imaginative flair, creativity and literary sensitivity at the service of his prose. No doubt his style was helped by his continuing interest in Greek and Latin literature. It was also honed by his wife, a writer of detective stories. But in the end his style was – well – himself, and it was captivating.

The third characteristic of Farrer was the depth of his spirituality, his transparency to God. It is not necessary to have known him to know he was a man of personal holiness, it is there to see in nearly every line of his writing. When C. S. Lewis introduced an American edition of his sermons he began by wondering why there were so few books like it. He ended:

> Perhaps, after all, it is not so difficult to explain why books like this are rare. For one thing, the work involved is very severe; not the work on this or that essay but the life-long work without which they could not even have begun. For another, they demand something like a total conquest of those egoisms which – however we try to mince the matter – play so large a part in most impulses to authorship. To talk to us thus Dr Farrer makes himself almost nothing, almost a nobody. To be sure, in the event, his personality stands out from the pages as clearly as that of any author; but this is one of heaven's jokes – nothing makes a man so noticeable as vanishing.

There are intellectuals who love the chase of ideas for their own sake. Farrer was not one of those. There are writers of genius at the mercy of their personal prejudices and foibles. Farrer was not like that. His razor-sharp mind and fecund imagination were put at the service of God as he has revealed himself in Christ. It is in this combination of intellect and imagination suffused with a deep spirituality that his genius lies. He would of course himself have dismissed the idea that he was a genius. The one genius, he would have said, is to seek the will of God and do it.

Farrer was a unity. It is therefore very difficult to split his life up into compartments labelled philosopher, biblical scholar, writer, preacher or pastor. He was of a piece. When I was a student at Cuddesdon Theological College in 1962 Farrer came to give some Holy Week lectures on the atonement. He came swiftly, if diffidently, up the aisle, a slight, abstracted figure. Then, unannounced and without any preamble, he talked aloud to God for the allotted hour before ending in as matter of fact a manner as he had begun. For one listener it was like having piece after piece of an intellectual puzzle put together. I sat and listened to a stream which flowed with utterly fresh and satisfying answers to barely formulated questions. Yet, at the same time, it was a kind of eavesdropping on someone thinking aloud to their God. As Basil Mitchell, a professor in Oxford at the same time as Farrer, put it:

> One had the impression that as he grew older his intellectual and devotional life and his practical activities became steadily more unified and his habitual mode of expression at once more simple and more individual . . . There was no discernible difference of tone between preaching and lecturing or between lecturing and everyday speech. Even the sustained eloquence of his Bampton Lectures was no more than the natural and unaffected expression of a unified intellectual and spiritual vision. Yet surely St Mary's had seen and heard nothing like it since John Henry Newman occupied that pulpit.

The final result of Farrer's fusion of qualities, of his particular genius, is rather startling for those of us in the twentieth century. For it found its most appropriate outlet and most perfect form of expression in the sermon. Hardly less thought went into his sermons than into his philosophical lectures. Indeed each sermon was the ripe fruit of a lifetime's meditation. As C. S. Lewis wrote, 'In each of them there is matter out of which some theologians would have made a whole book.' Above all the sermon form enabled Farrer to use his poetic imagination. But this imagination was not artificial or rarefied. It was related all the time to Farrer's own personality. As John Austin Baker, now Bishop of Salisbury, put it:

> It is by now generally acknowledged that Austin Farrer was one of the great preachers of his generation – indeed some of us would say, of any generation. In an age when rhetoric is mistrusted, he developed a new kind . . . His style was concrete, articulate, often beautiful, but above all acceptable, because it was suffused at its best with a delicacy that could be sensitive or light hearted as the time required. It was a quiet, sometimes self-mocking rhetoric; but a rhetoric none the less.

Then, his sermons enabled Farrer to be the Christian disciple and pastor. They ended on severely practical points about the use of money, on chastity, working for examinations, making up quarrels with parents and buying an alarm clock in order to wake up in time to go to Holy Communion. No vagueness there. For Farrer knew that the besetting sin of religion is unreality, what he called double thinking and what others might call pious and hypocritical make-believe. Farrer believed we only know God if we actively seek his will for our lives. And although strong on personal virtues that are less in fashion today he was highly sensitive to the real questions posed by the intellectual climate of our time. Although he rarely alluded to current controversies by name he is as often as not in his sermons wrestling with the issues in a way which combines intellectual lucidity and spiritual profundity.

Is Farrer easy or difficult? Some of his early philosophical and biblical writing is certainly difficult and virtually nothing of it has been included in this anthology. Yet most of his later writing has a surface simplicity. Much of it attracts and sparkles. Nevertheless, having read it, we can never be sure we have grasped all there is in it. Some passages of Farrer I must have read thirty or forty times and each reading has brought more to light. The pattern of Farrer's sermons is always the same. They begin with some odd or amusing everyday incident told in a straightforward conversational style. They end some ten minutes later in an inspired invocation of the majesty of God. It was impossible later, commented Basil Mitchell, to remember how the transition had been achieved. Farrer's hearers had been led from the world to God by being enabled to share in his own meditation. There was no conscious attempt to carry them away, no laying siege to the emotions, no difference of tone between the sermon and his everyday speech. But something had happened. Another colleague of Farrer's at Oxford, Leslie Houlden, describes the effect well.

He knew that if theology did not sail towards poetry, it may as well stay in the harbour. So preaching gave him his head. There imagination and artistry came into their own as the impulse of speech. Yet it is theology from start to finish, intellectually uncompromising, cutting no corners, facing the hearer with the plainest Christian truth. But was ever such doctrine so coaxingly conveyed? He woos us with his pictures, his flights of fancy – then, before we quite know it, we have seen the deepest things of faith under new illumination. The trap works perfectly.

Clearly the short extracts in this anthology cannot cast the spell that his full sermons obviously did for his hearers. But the hope is that something of the magic comes across. Certainly there are many insights, uniting thought and faith, that most of us have not yet grasped, or grasped fully, whose pondering will enrich the life of the spirit.

Richard Harries
King's College, London

March 1986

Editor's Note

This anthology has been arranged so that there are three readings for almost every week of the year. In addition there is a reading for each of the festivals and major saints days.

Whatever time of year a person begins to use this anthology or whatever church calendar he or she normally follows the hope is that the anthology will prove useful for reflection and prayer. For the readings have been chosen on their merits, to stand alone. However, it is also hoped that these readings might be of particular use to those who use The Alternative Service Book of the Church of England. There is here a theme of the week, derived from the ASB Sunday theme, which provides a loose focus for the week's readings. Whilst most parishes in the Church of England now use the ASB many people find the themes of the readings thin or constricting. Farrer's writings give these themes theological and philosophical depth. With him they take on real substance, so that those who preach or meditate on them find illumination for the mind and a challenge to the will.

Works Quoted

The Brink of Mystery, ed. Charles C. Conti. London: SPCK 1976.

A Celebration of Faith, ed. Leslie Houlden. London: Hodder and Stoughton 1970.

'The Christian Apologist', *Light on C. S. Lewis*, ed. J. Gibb. New York: Harcourt, Brace and World 1966.

The Crown of the Year: Weekly Paragraphs for the Holy Sacrament. London: Dacre Press 1953; New York: Morehouse-Barlow Co. 1953.

The End of Man, ed. Charles C. Conti. London: SPCK 1973; Grand Rapids, Mich.: William B. Eerdmans Publishing Co. 1973.

Faith and Speculation. New York: New York University Press 1967; London: Adam and Charles Black 1967.

Finite and Infinite: A Philosophical Essay. 2nd edn, 1958 reprint. New York: Seabury Press 1979.

The Freedom of the Will. 2nd edn, London: Adam and Charles Black 1963; 2nd edn, New York: Charles Scribner's Sons 1960.

The Glass of Vision. London: Dacre Press 1948.

Interpretation and Belief, ed. Charles C. Conti. London: SPCK 1967.

Lord I Believe: Suggestions for turning the Creed into Prayer. 2nd edn, London: The Faith Press 1958; New York: Morehouse-Barlow Co. 1959.

Love Almighty and Ills Unlimited. New York: Doubleday and Co. 1961; London: William Collins and Co. 1962.

'Messianic Prophecy and Preparation for Christ', *The Communication of the Gospel in New Testament Times*, Theological Collections 2. London: SPCK 1961.

A Rebirth of Images: The Making of St John's Apocalypse. London: Dacre Press 1949; Gloucester, Mass.: Peter Smith 1970.

Reflective Faith: Essays in Philosophical Theology, ed. Charles C. Conti. London: SPCK 1972; Grand Rapids, Mich.: William B. Eerdmans Publishing Co. 1974.

Said or Sung. London: Faith Press 1960; under title *A Faith of Our Own*, New York: The World Publishing Co. 1960.

Saving Belief. London: Hodder and Stoughton 1964; New York: Morehouse-Barlow Co. 1965.

A Science of God? London: Geoffrey Bles 1966; under title *God is not Dead*, New York: Morehouse-Barlow Co. 1966.

The Triple Victory: Christ's Temptations according to Saint Matthew. London: The Faith Press 1965; New York: Morehouse-Barlow Co. 1965.

The most complete list of Austin Farrer's writings is contained in *For God and Clarity, New Essays in Honour of Austin Farrer*, ed. Jeffrey C. Eaton and Ann Loades, Pennsylvania: Pickwick Publications 1983.

A biography of Austin Farrer, *A Hawk among Sparrows* by Philip Curtis, was published by SPCK, 1985.

My God and my All
My beginning and my end
My sole and everlasting good
My God and my All.

Lord I Believe, p. 32

9TH SUNDAY BEFORE CHRISTMAS

Theme of the Week: Creation

———

God Makes the World Make Itself

When we contemplate the physical creation, we see an unimaginable complex, organized on many planes one above another; atomic, molecular, cellular; vegetable, animal, social. And the marvel of it is that at every level the constituent elements run themselves, and, by their mutual interaction, run the world. God not only makes the world, he makes it make itself; or rather, he causes its innumerable constituents to make it. And this in spite of the fact that the constituents are not for the most part intelligent. They cannot enter into the creative purposes they serve. They cannot see beyond the tip of their noses, they have, indeed, no noses not to see beyond, nor any eyes with which to fail in the attempt. All they can do is blind away at being themselves, and fulfil the repetitive pattern of their existence. When you contemplate this amazing structure, do you wonder that it should be full of flaws, breaks, accidents, collisions and disasters? Will you not be more inclined to wonder why chaos does not triumph; how higher forms of organization should ever arise, or, having arisen, maintain and perpetuate themselves?

Though a thousand species have perished with the mammoth and the dodo, and though all species, perhaps, must perish at the last, it is a sort of miracle that the species there are should have established themselves. And how have they established themselves? Science studies the pattern, but theology assigns the cause: that imperceptible persuasion exercised by creative Will on the chaos of natural forces, setting a bias on the positive and achieving the creatures.

Saving Belief, pp. 51, 52, 53, 54

2

The Screen of Materiality

God's desire was to create beings able to know and to love him. Yet, in the nature of the case, there lay a dilemma. In proportion to their capacity for such love or knowledge, the created minds or wills would be dominated by the object of their knowledge or their love; they would lose the personal initiative which could alone give reality to their knowing or their loving. The divine glory would draw them into itself, as the candle draws the moth. You might say, 'Why should not he shade the light? Could not God put a screen between himself and his creatures?' But of what would the screen consist? A screen, literally understood, is a physical barrier; and it screens a physical object from an organ of physical vision. There cannot, admittedly, be a physical screen in the literal meaning of the term; for a screen must stand between physical senses and their physical objects; and even if God gives his creatures physical senses, he cannot make himself a physical thing. But suppose he creates a whole physical world, and places creaturely minds in it; suppose he so attaches them to it, that they are initially turned towards it, and find in it their natural concern. May he not then have strong animal minds, aspiring to know him in spite of their native physicality, instead of feeble spirits, whose obstacle lies in the mere poverty of their spirituality?

Might we perhaps say that the first requirement is to have a created world which is quite other than God? Then, by identification with such a world, godlike creatures may keep their distinctness from God, and not fall straight back into the lap of creating power.

Love Almighty and Ills Unlimited, pp. 69, 70, 71

God Works like a Good Novelist

The Creator of the world is not to be compared with those bad novelists who make up the plot of their story first, and force the characters to carry it out, all against the grain of their natures. He is like the good novelist who has the wit to get a satisfying story out of the natural behaviour of the characters he conceives. And how does he do it? By identifying himself with them and living them from within.

What is an impossible task for the human author is a constant achievement with the Author of Nature. He thinks all the natural processes at any level into being themselves and into running themselves true to type. And yet without faking the story or defying probability at any point he pulls the history together into the patterns we observe. The novelist who depicts the running of a business must manage it without reducing the office underlings to automata; he must allow them the free play of their personalities. God's creative thought must go deeper; while he thinks out the orderly life of a man's mind, he must at the same time think out the action of the minute physical underlings which carry the work of his brain, as they act out their own destinies according to their kind. If they are to do so, it must sometimes be that they rebel; the brain misfunctions or incurs damage, the purposes of thought are frustrated. Sometimes it must be so. Yet most of us are sane and capable most of the time, by Heaven's grace.

What moves believers to worship moves atheists to ridicule. A thought living at once on every level of natural process and thinking all levels into a single story is to believers the wonder of omnipotence and to sceptics the height of absurdity. Perhaps we cannot make those who come to scoff at us remain to pray with us. It will be something if we can help those who come to pray, pray with a more understanding adoration.

A Science of God?, pp. 76, 77, 78

4

8TH SUNDAY BEFORE CHRISTMAS

Theme of the Week: The Fall

=

Sin Is What I Do to God

To get sin out of the world I must get God out of the world, and I cannot. He is about my path and about my ways; his love is on the road before me, opening up those good works in which he predestines me to walk, and standing in the way of those follies to which I incline. I see that he opposes my wilful passage; I put my foot on the accelerator and drive through his opposition. Sin is what I do to God, wilfully violating his majesty and flouting his good pleasure. He meets me everywhere in so many forms, and specially in his breathing image, the human form divine. Again and again I trample him down. My sin is what I do to God; whether I am conscious of doing it or whether I am not, I do it; there it is, and if I become conscious of God I shall not remain unconscious of my sin.

Said or Sung, p. 58

5

Intolerable Pride

Innocent pride is positive, a glory in the use of talents, a promise of achievement. Bad pride is negative; it blinds us to truths of fact or even of reason, it disparages the achievements and hates the merits of others. . .

As against our neighbours, it will be enough if we allow them what we claim for ourselves. But such a degree of modesty is insufficient, when we face not our fellow creatures, but our common Creator . . .

For whereas pride in relation to our neighbours finds its check in the shock of our encounter with them, God is not so evidently encountered in this life; and the very pride which would be shattered by the vision of him is the reason why we fail to acknowledge him. Pride is a cause of blindness to our neighbours' merit: it is a cause of blindness to our creator's very existence, or anyhow, to his effective presence and his rightful sovereignty. What has happened? God displays his creative power chiefly in this, that he implants in his creatures an almost limitless energy of existence, and self-developing force . . . It is as though every sort of natural being were set to absolutize itself, and to be the whole universe if it can. Admittedly it cannot: its rivals check it. And it is out of this rivalry of physical self-assertions that God has been pleased to make the world. On the conscious and rational level, the creatures of God exult in a Godlike power, and fret against any limits set to the exercise of it. If we encounter God, we must recognize the very origin and institutor of our creative aspirations; but if we seem not to encounter him, but merely a feigned tale of a divine authority, we rebel against it in the name of the divine image we bear. To be converted is to repent our pride in dust and ashes, to see that we have so gloried in imported powers, as to deny and violate the majesty of glory itself. And after our conversion, we have constantly to acknowledge in ourselves and to wonder at the arrogance, which dares still to live by the choice of its own will, and so seldom even to consider the good pleasure of a compassionate and self-revealing God.

A Celebration of Faith, pp. 47 and 50–1

Awareness of God and Consciousness of Sin

Our relation with God being inescapable, since we draw our very existence from him, it is not something we are free to let alone if we choose. We violate his will if we do not follow it, we are starved of our supreme good if we do not embrace it. Alienation from God is a positive misfunctioning, a frustration of our total aim. If we are not reconciled to God, we are spoiling the music, we are not just letting music alone.

But we have to observe that not all actively cacophonous throats are aware of the discord they create, and not all wills in conflict with the divine know themselves to be so. Consciousness of sin implies consciousness of God.

In former times there were people by the million who believed in a divine author of the moral law, and knew perfectly well that they were running away from him. The preacher could rub the sore of their sin, and point the path to its cure. But now, anyhow among the sophisticated, the method of arguing oneself out of theistic belief is so current that few men put up with the annoyance of believing in a God from whom they know themselves estranged. Why, they can buy peace of mind and self-deception on the first bookstall they pass. So acknowledgement of sin becomes typical of Christians, who know how to seek renewed forgiveness for it.

Saving Belief, pp. 95, 96

7TH SUNDAY BEFORE CHRISTMAS

Theme of the Week: The Election of God's People—Abraham

——

God's Plan for Us

If we believe in God at all, we must believe in his wisdom and foresight. God does not push his creatures into existence like ducklings into a pond, to sink or swim and to fend for themselves. He has a plan for them. His plans for us are what perfect wisdom suggests to infinite love; his plans for us are his love, they are all the good that his love can see for us; as a parent's plans for his child would ideally be - he looks at the child and loves it, and in loving it sees what opens out before it.

New every morning is the love, and new every hour the loving foresight, which sees the openings for our happiness, and sets the opportunities of good ready to our hand. Reach out and take them, for now is the appointed time. God's plan is not a five years plan, but a five minutes plan; or, again, from another point of view, neither a five years plan nor a five thousand years plan, but a plan for our eternity, starting here.

But that is not all. Not only does God's wisdom continually open our path before us, God's grace is continually offered us for strength to walk in it. When I say to God 'I was weak', he says 'Why did not you ask my aid?' I could have done that: he reads my heart, and I have no answer, except that Christ has died for me to be forgiven. . . There is a divine intention for me, a path under my very feet, and there is divine grace by which to walk in it; and none of this is anything foreign or harsh, nothing forced upon me; it is all my own happiness, my only true good . . . Divine goodness has persuaded me, hedged up my path, headed me off, driven me back into the road; that is why I am here. I suppose it is abstractly conceivable that I could have been a greater fool than I was, but that is no reason for saying that I have been brought here by my own wisdom. 'You, O Lord, have wrought all our works in us,' the Christian must say.

Said or Sung, pp. 18, 19, 20, 21

8

Faith is Natural

We are all familiar with regions of intelligible fact which are only perceptible in the sunlight of a favourable attitude. Sympathy does not create the personal facts it descries, it reveals them; and there are many true facts sympathy appreciates, to which suspicion closes our eyes. I am not denying that sympathy lies open to imposture, or that suspicion is a necessary guard. I am saying what everybody knows – that the place of suspicion is secondary and subsequent. Without the initial venture of sympathy, suspicion has nothing material to criticize . . . To speak of sympathy for God would, indeed, be an impertinence; we may however dare to speak of openness, or acceptingness towards God.

But is it not a cruel and an unjust fate which makes the acknowledgement of God depend upon the forthcomingness of faith? . . . Yes, if faith were a capricious visitant; no, if faith is natural. The knowledge of humanity which is supremely worth having is denied to cynicism and mistrust; no one calls this an injustice, because sympathy is natural, mistrust and cynicism are vicious. That is not to deny that some men are so warped by circumstance, that they are cynical or mistrustful by no fault of their own. And so it is true that many men are incapable of faith. They can be cured, however, and God will cure them, whether in this life or hereafter. The corruptions of faith herself are so many and so appalling as to allow atheism to pass for illumination. But the aversion from faith need not be motived by faith's corruptions. Men turn from faith, because to acknowledge God is to acknowledge *my God*, and men either hate, or fear, to admit that they have a God, or that there is any will sovereign over their own.

Saving Belief, pp. 23, 24, 25, 26

God's Plan and Our Freedom

To say that we are predestinated to salvation and to say that our salvation is planned is to say the same thing: and no one can complain that the idea of planning is a stranger to the world in which we live. There are, indeed, two sorts of plans – there are western plans and there are eastern plans. Eastern plans tend to be ruthless, to handle humanity as mere material; they are something done to men, rather than anything that men achieve. Western plans are elastic, they are mere assignments for free agents to fulfil; as a result, they tend not to be carried out. There is a dilemma here, which it is difficult to resolve. When men plan for their fellow men, either they make the plans fit tight, and then they strangle the men; or else they let the plans hang loose, in which case the men get out of hand. But when God plans for men, it is not like this. His plans for us are close, not loose, they fit us like a glove; for the thought of God goes with our every motion, divine care clothes us like the atmosphere. And yet, his thought for us does not constrain us; what he designs for us is that we should freely act; what he creates is liberty. To enter into God's plan for us is to be most sovereignly ourselves; it is through giving us the power and courage to be ourselves that he fulfils his purposes in us. We can do nothing positive which does not give effect to everlasting love; the more creative we are (if we must use this arrogant word) the more we give expression to his will; for he is the sole creator, and to create through us is his design.

We cannot escape from God, any more than we can escape from the atmosphere; but then we do not want to; for why? we should cease to breathe . . . When we awake from sleep, we are present with him; for his designs open out in front of us before we have opened our eyes; they spread through the opportunities of the dawning day, and take shape in the good works he has created for us to walk in them.

The Brink of Mystery, pp. 98, 99

10

6TH SUNDAY BEFORE CHRISTMAS

Theme of the Week: The Promise of Redemption—Moses

==

The Consuming Presence

Moses at Mount Sinai implored God to leave, as it were, his throne on the mountain-top where the volcanic fire blazed and to come down into the camp of Israel and accompany their wanderings. The divine voice gave him many stern warnings before consenting. 'I cannot go up in your midst; for it is a stiff-necked people.' But at length the prayers of Moses, or rather the love of God, prevailed: 'My presence shall go with you, and I will give you rest.' Forthwith the voice began to teach Moses how God's terrible holiness could be housed within the camp without the sheer destruction of sinful men resulting. They were to prepare a special place, a travelling sanctuary, and fence it round with sanctity, and approach it with wariness and ritual precaution.

The presence of God was strength: Israel could not endure to lack him; but the presence of God was terror, and Israel could not endure to have him. 'We are killed, we are killed', they complained, when contagious sickness broke out in the camp as though the fire of God's presence had blazed out from the sanctuary in indignation at their sins. And so they set a fresh barrier between themselves and God. They chose one of their twelve tribes and made its members specialists in holiness.

Christ did not take anything away from the holiness and majesty of God, he just took away all the barriers which fenced the sanctuary. When he died on the cross, say the evangelists, the veil of the temple was rent to pieces; whether in physical or only in spiritual fact, I do not know. But anyhow the barrier went, and the presence of God is no longer in a safe enclosure, looked after by priestly experts in sanctity: we are all priests and God is lodged in us; the New Testament says, in our actual bodies.

The Brink of Mystery, pp. 14, 15, 16

11

Manna from Heaven

The minister at the altar still uses the ancient attitude of prayer; he holds out the palms of his hands, like a child waiting for you to throw him a ball, or like a man going out to feel the falling rain after a great drought. The bread of God falls like the manna from heaven; bring out your baskets, hold out your arms. God will fill your empty vessels if you will uncover them. You who come to this sacrament, what are your wants? Open the gulf of your desire, that God may fill it. Who desires holiness, who desires to care more for others than for himself, who hungers and thirsts for the Spirit of Jesus Christ? Ask, he says, and you shall receive, but ask.

The Crown of the Year, p. 42

Experimental Acquaintance with the Work of God

The will of God is in truth perfectly one, there is no rift or conflict anywhere in it. But we men in our attempts to think about it are bound to distinguish two strands in it, which God is, as it were, at pains to reconcile. There is his will for everything to be itself and act according to its kind, and there is his will for all things to work together towards further purposes. The first of these wills is, in a sense, basic, for everything must exist and be itself before it can serve any further purpose whatever. So the second will respects the first, and supplements it without violence to it, by a sort of persuasive pressure; and such is the divine will which takes effect through good men in their good actions.

Brute things are subject to the creative pressure, but being brute, cannot know they are. Enlightened men can not only coincide with its dictates, they can put themselves at its disposal. There is a union of wills in which God's will is inevitably directive and superior. Godly men know what they are doing; God's disposal of them becomes, through their association with its action, their experimental proof of religion. Let us paraphrase St Thomas. 'Experimental science concerns things we can work. But God is not to be worked by us. On the contrary, we men are his work', not only in our physical being, but more transparently in our moral existence. Nevertheless (we will now add) by associating our wills with his working of them, we acquire experimental acquaintance with the work of God.

A Science of God?, pp. 105, 106

13

5TH SUNDAY BEFORE CHRISTMAS

Theme of the Week: The Remnant of Israel

——

His Fingers upon Us

The skill of the divine potter is an infinite patience of improvisation. No sooner has one work gone awry than his fingers are pressing it into the form of another. There is never a moment for the clay, when the potter is not doing something with it. God is never standing back and watching us; his fingers are on us all the time. The world is his, from every side he touches and presses us. If we love his will we take the shape of it. If we are lazy and selfish, his fingers oppose us and make war on us, and crumble us back into obedience. We repent, and without a moment's delay the ever-active fingers are moulding us back into the divine image.

Said or Sung, pp. 80, 81

The Offering of Ourselves

The alms for which your generosity is asked are nothing exterior to the sacrament, but a part of it. If you were living in the days of the ancient Church, you would be bringing not money, but cakes of bread and flasks of wine. All would be placed upon the altar; part would be consecrated for the Eucharist, the remainder would be given to the sick and poor. Now you bring money. But your money is still presented along with the bread and wine, and it still means the same thing. The offering is your offering; it is you yourselves who are laid on the altar to be consecrated, and to be made the body of Christ. Your gift is a token of yourself. I break the bread for the death of Christ, and we are all sacrificed to God in Christ's death, dying in him to our own will, and receiving Christ our true life in communion.

The Crown of the Year, p. 43

As in the Days of Noah

Noah had the faith to believe divine warning, and the energy to act upon it. And until we can do better ourselves, let us throw no stones at Noah, or at his boat. For a higher authority repeats the warning: 'As it was in the days of Noah, so it shall be in the days of the Son of Man: they ate, they drank, they married and were given in marriage, until the flood came and took them all.' What was their crime? Just frivolity: for all the world like undergraduates, they kept up an endless party, and flirted with the females. Harmless so far as it went; but there was no future in it: the tides and currents of time have washed out the very trace of them. And so it shall be, in the day of the Son of Man.

What seems inadequate about Noah is his acting throughout from motives of fear and prudence. But in the gospel it is not like this. Christ is unsparing to his disciples in warning them of the destruction which awaits selfishness. Again and again, he touches the nerve of fear. And yet fear is only a preliminary motive, and to shrink back from the abyss is not to find the true path: it raises the question, it does not supply the answer.

To think of the day of judgement, or of death, is a motive of fear: I may die tomorrow; what, then, shall I do today? Not flog myself into some wonderful achievement, either of virtue or success: not write a poem, nor climb a mountain; nor even live a model day, controlled by all the rules I have often wished to keep. No: but look into the faces worthy of love, and see how dear; look, if I can look, into the divine countenance, under whose sunshine we walk, and do not know it; remember my absent friends, and see if anyone needs me; and if no human person, then what I can do to express my gratitude to the divine. For if the day of judgement, or the waters of Noah, had engulfed the Samaritan leper while he made his thanksgiving to Christ, and that had been the last use he made of his breath, he could scarcely have made a better.

The Brink of Mystery, pp. 78, 79

ADVENT 1

==

Hopes on Earth and Hope for Heaven

A Christian believer has two levels of hope. There's hope on the short view, hope within the world, that something can be made of it. But beyond that there's hope in the long view; hope that what we do in this world is not all going to leak out of the pipe of history into the sands of oblivion. So there are two levels of hope: and how stupid, how perverse it is to set them against one another: to say, 'Well, you must make up your mind; either fix your hope on this world, or fix it on a world to come. If you fix your hope on heaven, you'll not care a pin about the world's future; if you care about the world's future, you won't give a straw for heavenly bliss.' Nonsense: we are confronted with no such choice. Heaven alone gives final meaning to any earthly hopes; and to take it the other way round, we have no way to grasp at heavenly hope, than by pursuing hopeful tasks here below.

A Celebration of Faith, pp. 118, 119

God's Promise of Immortality

It is absurd for any Christian to undertake a defence of God's good providence, or to justify his tolerance of the evils he permits, without speaking of a resurrection. 'Come now,' says a sceptical antagonist, 'the resurrection of the dead is the supreme improbability. You can't expect me to consider that, until you have shown me the prevalence of divine goodness in human affairs apart from any such hopes. Bar out the life to come, and strike the balance of God's dealings with mankind, without it.' Shall I take up the challenge? I might as well agree to box with my wrists tied. How am I to strike the balance of God's dealings, if I leave out that single weight outweighing all which he has flung into the scale, his own godhead clothed with flesh, drawing us into the fellowship of immortal being? We cannot interpret the ways of God if we falsify them; and it never was his purpose to let perish any creature in which his likeness was so far realized, as to make the immortalization of such a creature meaningful. Immortal dogfish are no more to be looked for than immortal dogroses. But where there is a mind able to abstract itself from the mere concerns of its body, and to take its stand, as it were, on the steps of the all-surveying Throne; a mind able to look out through the impartial eyes of God, to share his concern for the common good of his creatures, and to love the fountain of that good in God himself; where there is a mind capable of such things (and the capacity is in all of us) it was never the purpose of God to let such a mind perish, unless it were through its invincible perversity. So we will not dream of justifying God's ways with men, if we are obliged to leave out of view the very highroad of his goodness, immortal hope.

Saving Belief, pp. 55, 56

Building Up Christ's Mystical Body

If it be asked what the Church is for, supposing men can be saved as well without a knowledge of Christ in this life, various answers can be given. The first and most obvious is that the mercy of God desires to redeem as many souls as may be redeemed in this present existence; and by means of the Church to make the force of Christ felt even where he is not adored. The second answer is that the divine society must really and directly be built upon earth out of earthly materials. If it exists, it can welcome and assimilate multitudes from outside; otherwise there would be no heaven into which they might go; for heaven consists essentially of its citizens, not of jasper bulwarks, or pavements of transparent gold. A heaven of souls without Christ would not be heaven; could we not say the same about a heaven of Christ without souls? Christ is not only God in man, he is God in mankind; God in one man isolated from all others would not even be God in man, for a man in isolation is not a human possibility. Christ's incarnation would have been nothing, but for his relation to his family, his disciples, and his nation; his continued incarnation after he rose would have been nothing but for his continuing relation with those he left on earth. Presently they joined him, one by one, in glory; and so that mystical body was built up, the nucleus of heaven, and the instrument of universal redemption. If those who know Christ in this life begin to complain, because multitudes who do not will one day be made equal with them, we know what Christ thinks of their attitude; it was one of his themes when he walked in Galilee, and taught his companions by his parables.

Saving Belief, pp. 156, 157

ADVENT 2

===

Seeing Christ in the Old Testament

The whole power and glory of the sun is in the sun, but gathered and concentrated in such a simplicity of incandescent splendour as to baffle our eyes. We turn from the sun, and range over the variety of his innumerable effects, the universe of warmth and growth and light. We gather and collect our impressions, we carry them back and up into their source, and so we enrich our perception of the power of the sun. And thus it is with our knowledge of God through the works of nature . . .

So it is again with the many figures of messianic anticipation and the one Christ. Christ has the intense and blinding simplicity of God . . . Here is too much light, too much truth, too much reality drawn into a point. But it was never the intention of God that this blinding simplicity should confront the unprepared mind. He had extended and shaded and scattered the truth of Christ in the manifoldness of the messianic images; and those who saw and believed Christ were inspired to draw together into him all this universe of anticipated meaning. What had the promise of a new temple signified? What but the flesh of Jesus Christ, wherein God truly inhabited? Who else but he was the marvellous child, the token of deliverance and bearer of the name *God-with-us?* All the atoning blood that ever ran down under the altar of Solomon, what had it been but a shadow of the death of Christ? And so one could continue endlessly . . . We look upon the works of God to see God, not to prove him; and the primary purpose of the apostles, say of St Paul, when they looked into the Old Testament, was not to demonstrate Christ thence, but to see Christ there. Certainly when they saw Christ in the Scripture it had the force of evidence, for seeing, after all, is believing; and they laboured to show him to others there, that they too might believe. They gathered, or collected, Christ from the Old Testament by the light of the Holy Ghost, and they called upon others to submit to the same illumination.

Interpretation and Belief, pp. 25, 26

Christ in His Letter

Here are a million or so printed words, in which divine gold and human clay are mixed, and I have to take the gold and leave the clay. Is there clay everywhere mixed with the gold, does no part of the text speak with a simple and absolute authority? Indeed it does in some part, for some part of it is the voice and recorded action of Christ, and in Christ the divine does not need to be sorted from the human, the two are run into one, for here is God in human nature by personal presence. Christ is the golden heart of Scripture. Indeed, if he were not there, the rest would not concern me. Why do I read St Paul? Because he sets Christ forth. Why do I read the Old Testament? Because it is the spiritual inheritance Christ received, it is what he filled his mind with, it is the soil in which his thought grew, it is the alphabet in which he spelled, it is the body of doctrine which he took over and transformed. So whenever I am reading the Old Testament I am asking, 'What does this mean when it is transformed in Christ?' and whenever I am reading the New Testament I am asking, 'How does this set Christ forth to us?'

People will always ask why God gives us his truth in such a mixed form; just as they will always ask why God made the world such a mixed affair. And those who are looking for excuses to live without God will say that, until God speaks more clear, they cannot be bothered to listen; but people who care about God will listen to him here, because this is where he can be heard and because it's a matter of life and death. What is the Bible like? Like a letter which a soldier wrote to his wife about the disposition of his affairs and the care of his children in case he should chance to be killed. And the next day he was shot, and died, and the letter was torn and stained with his blood. Her friend said to the woman: The letter is of no binding force; it is not a legal will, and it is so injured by the accidents of the writer's death that you cannot even prove what it means. But she said: I know the man, and I am satisfied I can see what he means. And I shall do it because it is what he wanted me to do, and because he died next day.

Interpretation and Belief, pp. 12, 13

Using Our Spiritual Ears

There is a great difference between the inspiration God gives us and the inspiration he gave St Paul. I do not merely mean that St Paul's inspiration was stronger than ours, or that he obeyed it more completely, though no doubt both those things are true. I mean that what he was inspired to do was something different. We are inspired to care for good things and to do good actions; we are not inspired to speak to our fellow men the words of God, as St Paul was. We may be inspired to embrace what St Paul revealed: he was inspired to reveal it. We may be inspired to expound what he taught: but he was inspired to teach it. Inspired, not manipulated: he spoke for God and he remained himself.

But if so, surely the practical result for the Bible-reader remains perplexing . . . If God inspires St Paul to speak, how are we to strain out St Paul, so as to be left with the pure word of God? We do not want St Paul's national prejudices or personal limitations, which, good man as he was, he could not wholly escape; no one can, it is like trying to jump off one's own shadow. How then are we to draw the line between the Apostle's oddities and the word of God?

If would save us a lot of trouble if we could find a cut-and-dried answer to that question; but cut-and-dried answers to spiritual questions are always false, and in the special matter of understanding God's word Christ rules such answers out. 'He that hath an ear to hear, let him hear', said he. We cannot hear the voice of God in Christ's words, let alone in St Paul's or Isaiah's, unless we have an ear attuned. After we have done our best to understand the words by the aid of mere honest scholarship, there is still something to be done, and that is the most important thing of all: to use our spiritual ears. If we do not believe that the same God who moved St Paul can move us to understand what he moved St Paul to say, then it isn't much use our bothering about St Paul's writings.

Interpretation and Belief, pp. 10, 11

21

ADVENT 3

―――

The Human Desire for Christ

What we are saying is this: that if Christ is for the human race, then the human race must desire Christ; and if they desire him, they will stay their hunger with idolatries. Idolatry will provide its own disillusionment; and this will be a world-wide preparation for Christ. The materializations of divine presence, the Bethels of idolatry, are not all equally ugly or grotesque; some of them are lovely enough and seem, in Christian eyes and after the event, to be poignant symbols of the incarnate truth. Nor is it so that all the Bethels of the Gentiles are, considered as such, inferior to those of Israel; or that the religious institutions and ideas of the Greeks are all, piece by piece, more barbarous than those of the Hebrews. What advantage, then, has the Jew? – if we may quote St Paul's words in a different argument; and we may reply, still out of the Apostle's mouth: Much advantage on every side; and to begin with, that they were entrusted with the miracles of God. The advantage of the Jews – the uniqueness of the Old Testament – lies in the voice of prophecy; their sacred institutions were not dumb signs, pointing through their very crassitude to the divinity they failed to contain; they were speaking signs, through the prophetic voice, of that fulfilment to which they knew themselves as tending. . . .

The development of human culture just happened, and there were many aberrations, many blind turnings in the process. Viewing the history of primitive and barbarous religion with a neutral eye, we might wonder whether it does not belong in the main to the history of human absurdity, of which the scroll, heaven knows, is long enough. But the tree is known by its fruit. Christ has come, we have seen God and we cannot doubt; and looking back over the long preparation for him, we can see that the divine hand which fashions man through all the apparent chances of his destiny has made him a God-fearer and a looker for Christ. There is no reason anywhere in the nature of things why man should have been brought to this; the reason lies in the will and love of his Creator, who, in ten thousand centuries, drew him out of clay, signed on his countenance the similitude of God, and breathed into his nostrils the breath of heaven.

'*Messianic Prophecy and the Preparation for Christ*', pp. 7, 8, 9

22

God Thinks Things into Existence as They Are

It is a poor speaker of French who thinks in English and translates as he goes; the true master of tongues thinks as he talks. He is a Frenchman in France and a German in Germany; why, he may find himself dreaming in German or in French. The shape, the idiom of the Creator's thought is the very shape and idiom of his creature's existence. God's thought of man is human, for he thinks man as he is. . . . God's thought of lions is lionlike, and of sparrows sparrow-like; and elementary things that have neither life nor sense are thought and willed by him exactly as they are or as they go.

I am not denying that the mind of man is a better image of God's mind than the mind of a beast, not to say than the mindless striving of inanimate forces. Only the divine quality in the human mind is not its humanness but its sheer mentality: its power (a limited power, certainly) to escape from ways of thought which express the human attitude, and to see every sort of thing just as it is.

We are not utterly without a sense of how a cat or a dog experiences its world. Not utterly without, but the power is painfully limited in us. Not utterly without, for we have mind, and mind (so far as we have it) is divine. And God can think every created existence, just as it goes. Indeed it would neither go like that nor be like that, if God did not think it so.

God thinks things as they are and designs them to go the way they go. He does not impose an order against the grain of things; he makes them follow their own bent and work out the world by being themselves. It is no matter of regret to God that the universe is not a piece of streamlined engineering. It is meant to be what it is - a free-for-all of self-moving forces, each being itself with all its might, and yet (wonder of wonders!) by their free interaction settling into the balanced systems we know, and into the complexities whereby we exist.

A Science of God?, pp. 74, 75, 76

The Dance of Christ

The primitive Christians, in the clumsy art of their catacombs, depicted Christ as Orpheus, the fabulous musician whose rhythm none could resist, who danced the fawns out of the forest and the firs down from the hill. Mere heathenism, do you say? No, they had warrant for it; for what else did Christ say of himself? Speaking of the unresponsiveness of the Jews to his mission, and to that of John the Baptist before him, 'You are like children,' he said, 'sitting in the street, and complaining to one another: We have piped to you and you have not danced, we have mourned and you have not lamented.' Mourned, that was John calling to repentance; piped, that was Jesus dancing them into the kingdom of God with the music of everlasting joy . . .

The other night we were sitting in the theatre watching the ballet, and almost equally amazed at two things: the beautiful rhythmic freedom of the dancers, and the stolidity of the audience. Perhaps their hearts were dancing within them, but if so, you couldn't see it on their faces. As for the performers, goodness, what a pleasure it must be to reach such a pitch of art, and trust your limbs to float and twinkle through the lovely maze of movement! What a release, and yet at the same time what a control!

What a release, and what a control; and the marvel of it is, that the release and the control are not two opposite factors balancing one another, they are one and the same thing. Suppose there are a lot of you together wanting to dance; what is it that releases, that sets you off? A rhythm picked out, let us say, on a pipe and a drum. That was the old village dance music. That is what releases you, something to dance to; but what is it that controls you? Why, the very same thing; you dance to the music. The control is the release, the music lets you go, the music holds you.

Well now, perhaps you will see why drums and tambourines are illuminating parables of true religion. For the whole mystery of practical religion comes down to that familiar phrase of our daily prayer, 'whose service is perfect freedom'. God our control, and God our release.

Said or Sung, pp. 182, 183

ADVENT 4

——

When Did He Become Man?

The Son of God became man in Christ. We generally think that it happened on Lady Day, or perhaps at the first Christmas. And yet an embryo is but the seed of manhood, and infancy little more than the promise of it. Are children human, before they can speak? And when they have spoken, how long is it before their words or their wills are their own? Christ became progressively a man by everything he did or suffered, up to the peak of his maturity. Then, in the flower of his age, he died. When he died, his making was not finished; for what sort of a man was he to remain? Not the sort of man we are, nor the sort of man any of us have ever seen, but the sort of man we must each of us be one day by God's grace; not the man in flesh and blood, but the man in glory. And how was he to reach that state? How is anyone to reach it, anyhow while this world lasts? He must pass the dead point of Hades. The parallel rays of the sun, passing the lens of a burning-glass, are so deflected that they slope together and cross all in a single point, a point, ideally speaking, with no magnitude; which point being passed, they fan out again into a fresh cone. The cone spreads to light, and, were it unbroken by an obstacle, should expand to all infinity. Death, the annihilation of all we were, is the point of no magnitude into which our being must contract, if it is to expand into the flower of glory. This is the pinpoint, this is the needle's eye, which we must pass to enter the Kingdom of Heaven. Here the rich unloads his wealth, and the proud his state, yes, and the poor his skin and bones, to slip through into a better world.

A Celebration of Faith, p. 103

25

Of Angels and Men

Just think of those nightingales – those nightingales we heard, the scout-troop and I – for believe it or believe it not, I was a scoutmaster once. We camped at Whitsuntide in a sheltered valley by a pretty stream; the low rocky sides were overgrown with trees; and as soon as our lights were out, the whole place was shouting with nightingales . . . But the pleasure of the song was not in our ear alone; it was in the nightingales. Why should they sing, if they did not delight in it?.

They do not know that they are; and yet perhaps it is right to say that they exult in their existence, and have a simple delight in it; and in so far they praise the handiwork of God with an entire sincerity; for so the Lord himself delights in his works: he looks on all that he has made, and calls it very good. There is no praise so sincere as delight.

To go to the other end of the created scale, angels have been thought birdlike, rather unconvincingly so far as their anatomy is concerned. They may be thought birdlike more seriously in the simple abandon and entire singlemindedness of their praise. The song of the angels is not adulation, or a paying of court to heaven's king: it is sheer delight; delight, indeed, in the glory of existence: but being far beyond selfishness the existence in which they delight is the existence they share; and the glory, the joy of their life is this, that it is wholly shaped and moved by the wisdom and the love of God. For pure spirits, simply to delight is to delight in God, and to delight in him is to praise him: so cherubim are but nightingales made explicit.

We men fall midway between the nightingale and the cherubim. Like the birds, we can find a simple delight in making melody, and in many other pure pleasures, and not know in what it is that we delight . . . Or again, we may try to imitate the cherubim, and strike the root of our joy into the ground of truth; finding that blessed will through which evils are redeemed and sorrows overcome and rejoicing to be one with the world's salvation.

The Brink of Mystery, pp. 42, 43

The Bride of Christ

St John sees the city - he sees her as the Bride of Christ. The city, not the Christian soul, is the Bride; such is everywhere the testimony of Scripture. God loves us each, indeed, as each a child of his; but the godlike glory which shows him his very image, and makes it possible to speak of a wedding between the Son of God and us - this glory does not attach to what each of us individually is, but to the community of love we have with one another. The community of human love, consecrated by God, this is divine; this is the city, and it is our place in it which brings us all within the scope of the heavenly marriage.

(The reference is to Revelation 21.1-7)

The Brink of Mystery, pp. 9, 10

Divine Sonship

We cannot understand Jesus as simply the God-who-was-man. We have left out an essential factor, the sonship. Jesus is not simply God manifest as man; he is the divine Son coming in manhood. What was expressed in human terms here below was not bare deity; it was divine sonship. God cannot live an identically godlike life in eternity and in a human story. But the divine Son can make an identical response to his Father, whether in the love of the blessed Trinity or in the fulfilment of an earthly ministry. All the conditions of action are different on the two levels; the filial response is one. Above, the appropriate response is a co-operation in sovereignty and an interchange of eternal joys. Then the Son gives back to the Father all that the Father is. Below, in the incarnate life, the appropriate response is an obedience to inspiration, a waiting for direction, an acceptance of suffering, a rectitude of choice, a resistance to temptation, a willingness to die. For such things are the stuff of our existence; and it was in this very stuff that Christ worked out the theme of heavenly sonship, proving himself on earth the very thing he was in heaven; that is, a continuous perfect act of filial love.

The Brink of Mystery, p. 20

CHRISTMAS DAY

Not an Explanation but a Life

God does not give us explanations; we do not comprehend the world, and we are not going to. It is, and it remains for us, a confused mystery of bright and dark. God does not give us explanations; he gives up a Son. Such is the spirit of the angel's message to the shepherds: 'Peace upon earth, good will to men . . . and this shall be the sign unto you: ye shall find a babe wrapped in swaddling clothes, and lying in a manger.'

A Son is better than an explanation. The explanation of our death leaves us no less dead than we were; but a Son gives us a life, in which to live.

Said or Sung, pp. 27, 28

CHRISTMAS 1

Theme of the Week: The Incarnation / The Presentation

===

Our All-or-Nothing

Unless God has gathered himself out of his immensity, and come to me as man, I do not even know that he is God - not, that is, if by God you mean the object of a personal devotion. Does the God of mere theism love the souls of men? And if he does, how is it that he has left the immeasurable gulf between himself and us unbridged? We cannot go to him. His love for us is that he comes to us. So the divine incarnation is our all-or-nothing.

A Celebration of Faith, p. 88

Mary's Fulfilment

Mary bears Jesus Christ, she sees, caresses, holds him and enjoys him for her own. Jesus is what she was for, his being and happiness are her natural fulfilment, in caring for him she is most herself. Blessed above women is she in whom the pull of nature is one with the drawing of grace; for whom the embracing of her child is the embracing of our only, all-sufficient and everlasting good. God gives us one another as images of his glory, he gives Mary himself as the dear fruit of her womb.

Lord I Believe, p. 89

Born a Begging Child

The universal misuse of human power has the sad effect that power, however lovingly used, is hated. To confer benefits is surely more godlike than to ask them; yet our hearts go out more easily to begging children than they do to generous masters. We have so mishandled the sceptre of God which we have usurped, we have played providence so tyranically to one another, that we are made incapable of loving the government of God himself or feeling the caress of an almighty kindness. Are not his making hands always upon us, do we draw a single breath but by his mercy, has not he given us one another and the world to delight us, and kindled our eyes with a divine intelligence? Yet all his dear and infinite kindness is lost behind the mask of power. Overwhelmed by omnipotence, we miss the heart of love. How can I matter to him? we say. It makes no sense; he has the world, and even that he does not need. It is folly even to imagine him like myself, to credit him with eyes into which I could ever look, a heart that could ever beat for my sorrows or joys, a hand he could hold out to me. For even if the childish picture be allowed, that hand must be cupped to hold the universe, and I am a speck of dust on the star-dust of the world.

Yet Mary holds her finger out, and a divine hand closes on it. The maker of the world is born a begging child; he begs for milk, and does not know that it is milk for which he begs. We will not lift our hands to pull the love of God down to us, but he lifts his hands to pull human compassion down upon his cradle. So the weakness of God proves stronger than men, and the folly of God proves wiser than men. Love is the strongest instrument of omnipotence, for accomplishing those tasks he cares most dearly to perform; and this is how he brings his love to bear on human pride; by weakness not by strength, by need and not by bounty.

Said or Sung, pp. 34, 35

Personal Identity

Wherever the eye of faith looks in the created world it perceives two levels of action. There is the creature making itself, and there is God making it make itself. Jesus is not unique in the mere fact that the personal life or act of God underlies his action; for nothing would either be or act, if God did not thus underlie it. But the underlying is not everywhere the same or (let us rather say) the relation between the underlying act of God, and the created energy overlaid upon it, is not everywhere the same relation. In the case of mere physical forces, there is the highest degree of mutual externality between the two; it is natural enough to speak of God's action here as the action of a cause. In the case of rational creatures, there is more mutual penetration; the entry of the divine into the human may be called inspiration on the one side, and co-operation on the other. In the person of Christ the mutual inter-penetration is complete; it is necessary to talk of a personal identity.

Saving Belief, p. 75

CHRISTMAS 2

Theme of the Week: The Holy Family / The Light of the World

====

At Home with Us

You also desire to have him at home with you – but how much less you
desire it than he desires it! He desires it with the whole of himself, and
how great he is! You do not even desire it with the whole of yourself;
no, nor nothing near it. But even if you desired it with the whole of
yourself, how little that would be, or rather, not little but nothing,
compared with the *All* that is God.

God's presence, spirit, power and love are poured into your church,
into your bodies and your souls, like wine into cups, as much as they
will contain, and then overflows. All the room you give him, he will fill.
And how shall you make him room? How extend his temple? By the
faithfulness of your Christian living, by your Christian friendship one
to another, your Christian witness to your neighbours, the devotion of
your heart's prayer to God. By these things the dwelling of God's mercy
shall be extended, though his power fills all extent, and all his works
praise him with speechless voices, Father, Son and Holy Ghost.

The End of Man, p. 167

Let Daylight Shine

With candid eyes? O God, save me from myself, save me from myself;
this frivolous self which plays with your creation, this vain self which
is clever about your creation, this masterful self which manipulates your
creation, this greedy self which exploits your creation, this lazy self
which soothes itself with your creation; this self which throws the thick
shadow of its own purposes and desires in every direction in which I
try to look, so that I cannot see what it is that you, my Lord and God,
are showing to me. Teach me to stand out of my own light, and let your
daylight shine.

Said or Sung, p. 174

Humanity as a Social Fact

There is one aspect of Christ's true humanity which is not sufficiently remembered by Christians; and it is this, that humanity is a social fact: we need other men, to be human ourselves. What is our mind, but a dialogue with the thought of our contemporaries or predecessors? And what is our moral being, but a complex of relationships? You would be another man, if your friends, relations and *bêtes noires* were different: and your personal being is profoundly altered if you deeply love a woman and go on in that companionship.

But have you reflected that Jesus was that Jesus because of Mary and Joseph and the village rabbi, a man to us unknown: above all because of the disciples to whom he gave himself and the poor people to whose need he ministered? But for these people, he would have been another Jesus. To be a man, he must have them, and to continue a man (as he still indeed is) he must retain them. So the life of God, incarnate in Jesus, cannot be locked within his breast; it becomes a spreading complex of personal being, centred in Jesus, and annexing his companions. Though we are each but a minute cell in the social body of Christ, yet, taking us in the lump and in the gross, he is what he humanly is by his relation to us.

And now I shall give you a definition of heaven. Heaven is a state of being, to us unknown, such that the obstacles to one man's knowing a multitude of individuals are done away. Then Christ is himself through taking us all into his heart and we shall be ourselves by taking him to ours.

A Celebration of Faith, pp. 89, 90

The Fountain of Light

One function which the old priesthood had, loses its use in heaven –
the priesthood no longer puts God's name upon his people by blessing
in his name: 'The Lord bless thee, the Lord keep thee, the Lord lift up
the light of his countenance upon thee' – the prayer is no longer required.
God has lifted the light of his countenance upon them for, says St John,
they see his face: his name is on their foreheads: there shall be night no
more: they need no lamp-light, nor sun-light: for the Lord God gives
them light, from the joy of his countenance.

He extends peace to them like a river; the blessing of God bursts
from the foot of his throne in a flood of bright, inexhaustible water, and
flowing through the city on every side turns it into a garden of Paradise . . .

For, says St John, God is there. He is there not because he belongs
there (for he belongs nowhere, he has no place) but because he bestows
his presence there, he descends into their midst, bringing all the glories
with him. For the heavenly city is like the earthly church in this, that
it is made to be what it is by God's stooping down to it. God, who came
down into the womb of Mary, comes down from heaven in the glorious
man, Jesus Christ. The throne of God in their midst, says St John, is
the throne of the Lamb: the special presence of the Father there is his
presence with the incarnate Son: the face that we shall see is the face
of Jesus.

Therefore what St John says of the heavenly city is not a mere dream
of the future without a bearing on our present state. What makes the
city above makes the Church below, the descent of Jesus into the midst;
and all the glories which are a feast in heaven are a foretaste here. For
God is with us in our true Immanuel; and, to the eye of faith, the
boundaries dissolve between that world and this; when we lift our hearts
up to the Lord, and with angels and archangels and the whole company
of heaven magnify the Name, and drink the fountain of light, the
overflowing love of Father, Son and Holy Ghost.

The Brink of Mystery, pp. 12, 13

EPIPHANY

Seeing the Image of God in Every Person

According to Moses, God is jealous; he will have our love for himself;
he will not endure that we should worship any image. According to
Christ, God is generous; for he is content that the love we owe him
should be paid to his living images. Yet this strict jealousy and this free
generosity are not contrary to each other. For the image Moses prohibits
and the image Christ allows are not the same. The accursed image is
that which we make, the work of our hands; but the blessed image is
the image God makes or, rather, the image he begets. And this blessed
image you can love. Indeed in the worthy sense you can love nothing
else. There are many other things that you can covet, but nothing else
you can love, in the sense of 'love' which includes appreciation and
contemplation, and a prizing of what, in itself, the object of your love
is. Nothing can be thus loved except the image and handiwork of God.
And the light of the glorious gospel of Jesus Christ reveals the image of
God everywhere; for this gospel is able to relate everything to Jesus
Christ. He who has seen Christ can see the Christ in all men, and
distinguish the Christ in them from the devil that is in them. He who
has seen Christ can look with new eyes on the works of nature, and see
a glory greater than Solomon's in common weeds.

For this light of glory, this good news of Jesus the image of God,
shedding splendour on the world and making God everywhere present,
has one enemy, says St Paul. It cannot be hidden except for those whose
eyes the God of this world has blinded. Nothing blinds us to the true
and living image of God except the false man-made idol, worldliness.
He who is pushing his fortune sees not the creatures of God, but the
materials of his own designs. His friends are not possible Christs, but
useful contacts.

Said or Sung, pp. 49, 50, 51

EPIPHANY 1

Theme of the Week: The Baptism of Jesus

===

In You Is My Delight

John dissuades Jesus from being baptized, but he will not be dissuaded; he joins his people in dedication for what is to come. He has no sooner touched the dedicating waters, than it comes; the skies open, the Spirit like a spark of power flies from the heart of heaven to his, the Father's voice is in his ears: You are my beloved Son, he says, in you is my delight.

The Crown of the Year, p. 90

Groping Forwards

Christians have often been so overpowered by their sense of the divine presence in Christ, that they have seen him as no true man; a god in masquerade. But those whose imaginations have thus deluded them have been going flat contrary to the formal teaching of the Church, which acknowledges in Jesus Christ a manhood as entire as his deity. This was how God's love was shown as utterly divine – in accepting every circumstance, every limitation of our manhood. He spared himself nothing. He was not a copybook man-in-general, he was a Galilean carpenter, a freelance rabbi: and he wove up his life, as each of us must, out of the materials that were to hand. He found his way by groping and he knew his Father by trusting; only he made no false moves.

A Celebration of Faith, p. 89

The Father's Good Pleasure

He delights in goodness with all the delight there is, not because it is his, but because it is good. Indeed, self-love is always an artificiality or a perversion. God loves infinitely an infinite goodness; the Son loves it in the Father whence it comes, the Father loves it in the Son in whom he places it, and upon whom he pours it out: 'This is my Son, my only beloved, in whom I am well-pleased.'

The Father's unqualified delight, his outpouring of his Holy Spirit, comes down with Christ from heaven to earth and continues to enrich his mortal condition; only that now it is measured to him according to the need and experience of the day. The infant Jesus lacked nothing of what his little heart was able to receive; the growing boy was capable of more, the grown man of more again. Nor did it stop there; Jesus, more perfect in his manhood than any of us, was pre-eminent in the capacity for spiritual enlargement; and when he threw himself into the train of events which the Baptist set going, there was so much wider a field for divine goodness to fill, that the Spirit came down upon him like the breath of a new creation.

When St John came to write the story of Christ's baptism, he connected it with Jacob's dream of the ladder from heaven to earth, on which the angels of God ascended and descended (John 1.32, 51; Gen. 28.12). And certainly the Baptism has so many levels of meaning in it, that without ever going outside it we can run up as though by steps from earth to heaven and down again. At the height of it is the bliss of the Trinity above all worlds, in the midst is the sonship of Jesus to his Heavenly Father; at the foot of it (and here it touches us) is the baptism of any Christian. For Jesus when he stepped into Jordan became the example and the power of baptism; as Jesus rising from the dead is the resurrection and the life, so Jesus undergoing baptism is the regeneration by water and by Spirit. We cannot be baptized without being baptized into his baptism: and the unity we have with him both in receiving baptism and afterwards in standing by it, brings down on us the very blessing and the very Spirit he received. In so far as we are in Christ, we are filled with Holy Ghost, and the Father's good pleasure rests upon us; infinite Love delights in us.

The Triple Victory, pp. 32, 33

Knowing on Our Knees

If we lay down the dogma that Gospel history is just like any other history, we are committing ourselves to the proposition that Christ is just like any other man, or anyhow that his humanity is cut off from his deity and holds no communion with it. 'Who has known the mind of the Lord,' says St Paul, 'that he might be of his counsel?' . . .

The New Testament writings are perfectly clear, and perfectly realistic about this. This natural mind could not understand Jesus in his historical existence, not even the natural mind of his immediate companions. Nothing but the supernatural overflow of the mind of Jesus into them created that affinity whereby they could begin to understand him. Only God can understand God, even when God is incarnate. But God is in us by the Holy Ghost, and therefore we can know incarnate God. This is as true of us in our historical study, as it is of us at our prayers. We cannot know Christ in the history about him, except by the Holy Ghost.

In one sense, then, gospel history is just history, and its procedure is the same as any history's. It is the interpretation by sympathetic understanding of a web of interacting minds, with some of which, the evangelists, we are in immediate contact, with others, Christ and the Twelve, Caiaphas and Pilate, in a contact not in the same way immediate. So far gospel history is like any other history. It is different, because one of the minds, Christ's, is not merely a natural mind, and can only be understood, therefore, by a supernatural gift. There is therefore no neutral history of Christ common to unbelievers and believers. We either accept, or do not accept, the witness of the Holy Ghost. We understand the Christ who proclaimed himself the Son of God, because we understand, though but partly, what it is for Christ to be the Son of God. And we understand what it is for Christ to be the Son of God, because we perceive ourselves to be, in him, partakers of divinity. The God incarnate is not to us an unintelligible enigma, because our existence in grace hangs upon the fringes of his incarnation. We know, on our knees, and in the depth of our heart, what Christ is, by knowing what he has made us: and we know what he has made us, by knowing what he is.

A Celebration of Faith, pp. 44-5

EPIPHANY 2

Theme of the Week: The First Disciples

———

Placed in God's Hands

A Christian who knew his own heart might pray in some such fashion as this. My God, I wish to give you the gift you so much desire; I wish to commit myself to you once and for all, so there shall be no taking back. I cannot commit *myself* into your hands, O God, *I* cannot do it; but yet I can commit myself into *your* hands; for though I cannot keep myself there, your fingers can hold me there, your strong, gentle fingers always giving way and never letting go; your wise, subtle fingers, wrestling so gently against my puny rebellions, that I tire myself trying to climb out of your hands, and come to rest at last in those wounded palms. You will not let me go; for though I have not the virtue to commit myself to you by an irrevocable act, you have had the love to commit yourself irrevocably to us. I cannot nail myself to you past breaking loose, but you have nailed yourself to us, witness these wounds. Your voluntary self-oblation, begun by free choice, hardened into unalterable necessity when they sentenced you, when they nailed you, when they lifted you into the air alive yet fixed, incorporate with the dead wood, and stiffening through agony into the irreversible fixity of death. You gave, beyond taking back, you were committed, when you gave your spirit into your Father's hands; and so I am content to know that I am committed into yours. For you are our everlasting shepherd, with the Father and the Holy Ghost, one God; to whom be ascribed, as is most justly due, all might, dominion, majesty and power, henceforth and for ever.

Said or Sung, p. 146

The Completion of Christ's Incarnation

God could not become incarnate in a human vacuum, and neither can he remain incarnate so. How justly, then, are Christians called the members of Christ! It is not only that they cannot find their perfection, except by subordination to such a head. It is just as much that he cannot live as a human person, without his person being extended and expressed in such members as these. What we are saying has nothing to do with the heresy, or rather, the blasphemy, which declares us men to be necessary for the completion of the life of God. No; God need never have created us, nor, having created us, need he have redeemed us, nor, perhaps, need he have redeemed us by becoming incarnate in us. But since he has been pleased to become incarnate, he needs the stuff and the embodiment which are involved in a true incarnation; that is, he needs the mystical Church, with which he will appear on the Last Day.

The problem was how we were to reconcile two principles. First, heaven must be genuinely made out of earth, without forcing the natures of the earthly constituents; a process which seems impossible except through much prodigality or wastage of materials, the materials in this case being human souls. Second, salvation must effectively embrace all rational persons who are willing to have it in the shape in which God offers it. What, then, is the reconciliation or solution we propose? It is this. The highly selective or (as we have called it) wasteful process really takes place within the field of human history. But what this process is designed to effect is not the general salvation of mankind. It is the completion of Christ's incarnation. Christ is made whole in head and members; this is the Israel of God, the core and substance of heavenly being, a reality sufficient to act as the touchstone of judgement for all the souls of men, assimilating to itself and embodying in its own life those who are found able to respond – and none will be found unable but by their own fault.

Love Almighty and Ills Unlimited, pp. 129, 130

The Response of the Whole Person to the Whole Christ

The issue which faces us is to recognize true God when we see him. And what is the organ or faculty for recognizing God? The eyes for colour, the ears for sound, the method of logical thought to test an argument. But with what power shall God be recognized? With no single power, but with our whole life and being. Why, you cannot discover your true friends, or the wife you ought to marry, with less; so how should you discover God with less? It takes all of man to acknowledge man, it takes more to acknowledge God; it takes God, the Holy Ghost speaking in the heart. To believe in Jesus we must co-operate with the Spirit of Jesus, the Spirit wherewith Jesus has colonized our minds.

If you ask, then, 'Shall I not be able to talk away the evidence for Christ's godhead? Shall I not be able to make up plausible theories to account for everything without an incarnation?' I will reply, Yes, you will be able to talk it away; but God, when it pleases him, will show you that you are deceiving yourself by so doing. 'Well then,' you may say, 'but if I admit the evidence, need a miracle-worker be God?' I answer, No. 'Need a man who claims what Jesus claimed, be God?' I answer, No. 'A man appearing as risen from death?' No, and so with the rest. But what is the proper response of the will and intellect and the heart, to the whole evidence of Christ? That is the question which, once answered, has to be answered all over again in every vital decision of life.

Said or Sung, pp. 93, 94

41

EPIPHANY 3

———

The Religion of Delight

Christ attended a wedding. What, then, was Christ's concern – what is Christ's concern – in the weddings of his friends? We do not read that he laid down the law to them at that time, or told them their obligations – we read that he concerned himself with the supply of their wine. It seemed a shame to him, if anything was lacking that could spread abroad delight. The bride and bridegroom drank from the cup. They passed it round, and their friends tasted the very flavour of their joy. Christ would not bear to see the flow of happiness interrupted, for lack of wine in which to drink it.

Does this surprise you? Did you not expect Jesus to be the servant of natural delight, the abettor of warm-hearted pleasure? But have you forgotten what Christ is? He is the desire of nations, he is the joy of all mankind: he came to take away the cold religion of duty, and to substitute the religion of delight. We are to do our duty – yes, but we are to delight in it, for the love of our neighbour, and for the dear love of God. There is nothing else but this, that we can hope for in heaven itself – nothing but to do good unalloyed by any meanness, and to do it with infinite delight. And how shall we be able to do so? By feasting on the vision of a face, whose eyes are the deep wells of happiness and love.

It is not surprising at all, then, that Christ should begin his ministry at a wedding: for a true marriage is a special favour of God's grace, and a direct foretaste of heaven. God's glory is reflected, for those who truly love, in one another's faces; they see the creator shining through his handiwork, and the vision inspires them with a simple delight in doing one another good, and in furthering God's will. Those who are being married know what they want to do: and it is exactly what God desires them to do. They do not, as the rest of us so often must, make themselves care about the will of God: they do care for it: for they care for one another.

A Celebration of Faith, pp. 136, 137

Showing Our Need

But why use bodily miracles to teach us truths of the spirit? So far from miracles helping to explain, they are of all things the most in need of explanation. Why use miracles? Why, because we are miracle-lovers; and the first thing for us to get into our heads is that we are asking for miracles all the time. We Christians, like the bridegroom at Cana, are obliged to put on a party for mankind; we are bound to offer all comers divine fellowship and inextinguishable joy. And where's the wine? Aren't the supplies dry? What can we drain from the bottom of the barrel? Perhaps Mary will take heart and say for us, 'They have no wine.'

The first thing, then, is to realize that we want miracles, and that we do not know how miracles are to be done; a small point since it is not we who are going to do them. I find in myself this foolishness, that when I call in the aid of a workman over something I can't repair, I have to tell him what I think to be the cause of the trouble, and how it should be mended. The poor man is merely fogged by my suggestions; but at last I let him look at the bother for himself; a broad smile of intelligence spreads over his face, and his clever hands go to work. Why tell divine wisdom what to do? We have only to show our need.

. . . There is simple and immediate attention to our need as soon as it is known. Now to many of us this is the very touchstone of faith. Can you believe that every moment you have only to turn to Christ to be accepted with him?

The Brink of Mystery, pp. 156, 157

Glories Hidden and Revealed

O God, the glories are hidden; we have them by faith and by your word. Believing in you, we believe in your promises. And yet it is not one thing to believe in you, and something additional to believe in what you promise. For it is you that have promised, and if you had not promised, you would not be you; still less, if your promises failed of their fulfilment. For what are you to us, if you are not an Almighty Father, and what Father are you, if you do not bring your children home?

Even now we do not receive your promises as sounds in our ears lacking present effect. For the word and the Spirit by which you assure us of felicity to come are the beginning and foretaste of what they foretell. The order of grace in which our redemption has placed us is nothing but the fivefold reconciliation beginning to work; our present salvation is a first dawning of heaven. I do not know which of two things I ought to say – that we understand glories not yet possessed by the token of present mercies, or that we understand mysteries obscured in the darkness of our present state through their foreseen manifestation in everlasting light. Or shall I say both things together? For without the present tokens of your love, we should have neither taste nor sense of your glorious promises; and without the promises of glory, we should have no understanding of your present love. For this is your love, that you have taken us by the hand to lead us to yourself; and if you led us blindfold in this darkness without revealing to us the destination of our journey, we should not know in what your love essentially consists. But now we know, because he who is the Way says also that he is the everlasting Life of his friends.

Lord I Believe, p. 78

EPIPHANY 4

====

Clear Lines against the Sky

The new Temple is not wood or stone: like Jesus its foundation, it is alive. Hear what St Peter says: 'Coming to him, the living stone, ye also as living stones are built up into a spiritual house: for ye are a chosen race, a royal priesthood, a holy nation, a people of God's own possession, that ye may show forth the excellencies of him who hath called you out of darkness into his marvellous light.'

Why compare a mass of people to a temple? What is the sense of it? A temple is rigid, square, clear-cut, a visible block, bearing its purpose on its face, unmistakable for anything else: and unless it has these characters, it cannot witness to God. Pull the stones down and pour them back into the quarry; they may be excellent stones, they will not be a Church. And so with us, whom St Peter calls living stones. As a point of history, let me assure you of this: from the first moment of its foundation, the Church was hard, clear, visible, and firmly knit: nothing mossy about its edges. Its members professed one truth – they would not have risked death for religion, if they had not been convinced of the gospel. They submitted their lives to the congregation, under the leadership of the ministers whom Christ's Apostles had given them: if they were judged to have given scandal by their disloyal lives, they accepted penances from the Church, they fasted and wore mourning until they were readmitted to communion. They paid for the upkeep of the poor. They were present every Sunday at the Holy Sacrament: if they were absent, they were assumed to be sick: they were inquired after and the Holy Communion was carried to them. Their heathen friends divorced their wives if they were tired of them: the Christians did not. Their heathen friends could make money in any profitable line: the Christians were forbidden a whole list of dishonest or indecent occupations. Their heathen friends rose in the government service: not so the Christians, because of the idolatrous oaths and other ceremonies attaching to public office under Caesar. The lines were clear enough, sharp enough, and costly enough, which silhouetted the living temple of God against a heathen sky.

A Celebration of Faith, pp. 154, 155

The Rock of Truth

A tender heart will say, is it not vindictive of God to smash our falsities against the rock of his terrible truth? Why shouldn't he let us go? Let us go? But if our Creator lets us go, we shall undoubtedly perish. Our only life is to be reconciled to him; and we cannot be reconciled to him without being reconciled to truth. That degree of judgement, at least, awaits us all; we have got to see all the lie our life has been. We have got to see what we thought we were, and what we were, we have got to see what God designed us to be, and what we made ourselves to be. We have got to see the scars of our neglect or hardness of heart on our neighbours' souls. We have got to see what a God we have, and how we have used him. That is our purgatory. I do not know if it will be short or long. I am sure it can be shortened hereafter by present penitence. If there are any souls who can never reconcile themselves to God's truth, then in hell they are and in hell they remain.

But we will dare to hope that the very thing that makes our torment will be our joy and our salvation. What is it that will break our hearts, but the vision of the divine mercy which we have disappointed? And what will be our everlasting joy, if it is not that same mercy, full of forgiveness to us and happy to have borne the wounds of our cruelty, if, by bearing them, he can vanquish our enmity?

What is it, then? Our assurance of a life to come cannot be firmer than our assurance of God himself. If you believe that he has saved us, you know that he has saved us with an everlasting salvation; for no salvation that is not everlasting is any salvation at all.

The End of Man, p. 89

God in His People

If God were conveniently remote, we could believe in him, but the only God whom we know is not remote: he indwells us. And how can we believe in an indwelling God unless we manifest the effects of his indwelling? Our faith is destroyed, unless we really are the living and moving temples of God. But what are the facts? Our attention fixed nine-tenths of the time on our own selfish concerns; an occasional half-hearted prayer, every now and then a grudging consent to do God's will rather than our pleasure. Such is the life of most of us, and it destroys faith in the indwelling God through flagrant unreality . . .

Well, in the end we have got to earn our faith: we have got to become actual temples of God, and we have got to bring our eyes round and keep them on his face – not like the sinners whom God's prophet found in the temple of Jerusalem, with their backs to the sanctuary, worshipping the stars. We have to become God's temples, and his priests. But meanwhile we take refuge with Christ. For the reality of God's indwelling in man is not to be tested by our response chiefly. If we are God's temple where he dwells, we are not so individually only or in mere isolation. God dwells in his holy Church, of which we certainly are parts; but we are not the main substance of it. The Church of God is Jesus Christ and the saints chiefly: it also embraces us, for Christ embraces us. But the reality of God's indwelling is tested by his indwelling in Jesus Christ first, and then by the repetition and continual manifestation of Christ's life in the glorious saints. Here the evidence is plain enough: there is no unreality here.

But Christ and the saints do not stand like the old Jewish priesthood as a screen between the holiness of God and us. We cannot push the duty of being worthy of God's indwelling off on to them. God in his mercy treats us all as one: one body of Christ in which the holiness of Christ, the single-minded devotion of Christ, is found. We are all bound together in that glorious body: Christ's self-sacrifice for us, and his continual prayers for us, hallow us and spread holiness upon us. In like manner the saints pray for us, and we pray for one another. In this whole body of the holy Church God resides.

The Brink of Mystery, pp. 16, 17

EPIPHANY 5

Theme of the Week: The Wisdom of God

==

Unwisdom

We said that attentiveness and candour were the conditions of belief; but when it is religious belief that is in question, the attentiveness and the candour need to be exercised in the field of wisdom, if they are to bear upon the point. It would be odious to quote names, but some of our most renowned philosophers have seemed most unwise: have proved unable to manage their matrimonial affairs with happiness or even with tolerable dignity; or to handle their growing children with any marked success. Worse than that: they have sometimes seemed to be men of paper, for whom the universe is reduced to written propositions.

A Celebration of Faith, p. 69

More Good Reasons, Not Less

The trouble about an indiscreet belief in inspiration is that it smothers reason. A man who declares 'This is what the Spirit directs' is not required to give a reason; surely God does not argue his cases. But I say to you, always suspect claims to inspired guidance which bypass reasoned argument. There are not fewer reasons for what God ordains than for other things; there are more, far more. There are all the reasons in the world, if we can but find them. For is not he wise?

The End of Man, p. 64

God as the Mind of the World

God is the mind of the world - Yes, indeed, and that is how he differs from my mind which can never be more than the mind of me. True, I attempt to enter into the subjectivity of a limited number among my fellow-beings, but my power to do so is very imperfect; and even then I cannot become their mind, so as to cause or operate their proper action; it is theirs, not mine. But God is the Mind *of the World*, that is, he is not tied to any base of operation that is exclusively his; he enters fully into the subjectivity of all the world's constituents. What is more, he does not enter into them simply after the event, with a sympathy perfect, perhaps, but still impotent; he enters into them by prior causality, willing them the existence and the activity they exercise; and so he is indeed *the Mind* of the world.

To be the mind not merely of you or of me but of all creatures, God must be a free Spirit, whose action is prior to the actions of them all. . . .

By concerning himself with a plurality he unites it in the unity of his concern. The unity is the unity of the divine initiative. Only, in making even so innocent a statement as this, we need to be on our guard against the false suggestions of the human model. When a man confers a sort of unity on a miscellaneous collection of persons, animals and objects by giving them a place in his multifarious activities or interests, he does impose upon them a scheme of order which is his own, and alien to them. For the possible patterns of human interest or activity, though indefinitely numerous, remain specifically human. However varied, they are variations on set themes. Whereas it would surely be irrational to suppose in God a determinate nature, like that of a finite species, prescribing an order in his concern with things particular to himself and foreign to the things. Surely his concern for his creatures is for them to be themselves, or more than themselves; not for them to act as pawns in some specifically supernatural game which any divine hand is bound to play. A man's concern for his fellow-beings, however generous, must be a straitjacket compared with the openness of God's concern for the world.

Faith and Speculation, pp. 153, 154, 153

EPIPHANY 5

Spreading the Area of Recognition

Think of my mother, now – you have known women like her, though few, perhaps, as good – a more unphilosophical thinker it would be difficult to find. Now suppose that in the heyday of my adolescent intellectualism I had told her that she had no right to her fervent evangelical faith, not being able to put together half a dozen consistent sentences in justification of her mere belief in God. What would she have said? She would have told me that admired intellects had bothered themselves with such inquiries, and been able to satisfy their minds: for her part, God had given her faith, and God had never let her down except it was by her manifest fault.

. . . The centre of your Christian conviction, whatever you may think, will be where my mother's was – in your exploration of grace, in your walking with God. But faith perishes if it is walled in, or confined. If it is anywhere, it must be everywhere, like God himself: if God is in your life, he is in all things, for he is God. You must be able to spread the area of your recognition for him, and the basis of your conviction about him, as widely as your thought will range.

A Celebration of Faith, pp. 59, 60

EPIPHANY 6

Theme of the Week: Parables

===

Through a Glass Darkly

Now God is a reality as is our soul, absolutely present and active in the existence and operation of all the creatures; for they are the expression of continual creative power. But though we had the eyes of angels to see his work, though we enjoyed that vision of him face to face reserved for those who have put off mortality and passed the purging fire, our inability of speech would still remain. It is his uniqueness and not only his hiddenness, which prevents our saying anything perfectly exact about him, except that he is himself: that God is God alone; and the very hymn of the angels, Scripture divines, is not an expression of what he is by himself, but an appeal to the various similitudes in which the creatures share and imitate his being: *pleni sunt caeli et terra majestate gloriae tuae* ['Heaven and earth are full of the majesty of thy glory']. Of himself, they can only say that he is, and that he is exalted: 'Sanctus, Sanctus, Sanctus, Dominus Deus Sabaoth.'

It is therefore not a scandal, but something every hearer of poetry should understand, that all the statements we make about God are similitudes, as it is written, *per speculum in enigmate* ['through a glass darkly']. I will appear to man through a glass and *in a riddle*. All words about God pose a riddle . . . Let us call him the *eternal spirit*. That is as much as to say, 'Find a being in whom the living act of personality and the changelessness of mathematical truth meet and coincide.' The personal life that we know is above all in movement and changeable, and the eternal truth we know is neither personal nor alive, but God is the unimaginable being in whom these two are one. To object to such paradoxes is just to be silly and to ignore the point - the uniqueness of God.

Reflective Faith, p. 35

51

EPIPHANY 6

The Splintered Image of God's Existence

Every argument for God's existence must start from the world of finites, or from the nature of finite substances as such. And it must proceed from a distinction taken within the finite. 'If the world is, then God must be' may be true, but it is scarcely an argument. We must take some distinction within the finite and then claim to show that the coexistence of the elements distinguished, in the way in which they do coexist, is intelligible only if God exists as the ground of such a coexistence.

The argument, therefore, has first to exhibit the finite coexistence which is its base, and then to convince us that this coexistence demands the divine existence. In thus proceeding, it is bound to make a violent jump in the middle. For it will exhibit a coexistence of elements which is revealed by the analysis of the finite order, upon the level of thought which has the finite for its object, and by the employment of finite principles alone. But when the argument proceeds to exhibit the coexistence revealed by such analysis as demanding the existence of God, it makes a jump from the finite to the infinite plane; for it is only because we in fact see the finite coexistence as the splintered image of God's existence, that we regard the finite elements as not merely coexistent (which would be a fact demanding no explanation) but composite (and therefore requiring in the simple a ground for their composition).

The argument therefore exhibits a distinction of elements within the creature in order to make us jump to the cosmological intuition, i.e. to the apprehension of God as the being in whom this distinction is, in its finite form, transcended – who is the 'coincidence' of these 'opposites'. But how does the argument lead us to make this intuitive jump? It may be sometimes enough to state the distinction and its transcendence in God, for the hearer or reader to see the conclusion. But the further removed he is from theistic ways of thought, the less likely is this to succeed; for he will not see what is meant by the notion of this transcendence, and so it will be necessary to help him out with analogies.

Finite and Infinite, p. 262

52

Looking

I count poetical vision and even amatory passion the friends of religion, in spite of the fact that their abuse may easily tend the other way. But though poetry often breeds an attitude of fancifulness and egotism; and love, heaven knows, of animality and complacency; yet we have on the other side to set this – that the lover and the poet at least look at something and see it. And the chief impediment to religion in this age, I often think, is that no one ever looks at anything at all: not so as to contemplate it, to apprehend what it is to be that thing, and plumb, if he can, the deep fact of its individual existence. The mind rises from the knowledge of creatures to the knowledge of their creator, but this does not happen through the sort of knowledge which can analyse things into factors or manipulate them with technical skill or classify them into groups. It comes from the appreciation of things which we have when we love them and fill our minds and senses with them, and feel something of the silent force and great mystery of their existence. For it is in this that the creative power is displayed of an existence higher and richer and more intense than all.

Reflective Faith, pp. 37, 38

The Christian Imagination of C. S. Lewis

It was this feeling intellect, this intellectual imagination which made the strength of his religious writings. Some of those unsympathetic to his convictions saw him as an advocate who bluffed a public eager to be deceived,˙by the presentation of uncertain arguments as cogent demonstrations. Certainly he was a debater, and thought it fair to make the best of his case: and there were those who were reassured by seeing that the case could be made. But his real power was not proof, it was depiction. There lived in his writings a Christian universe which could be both thought and felt, in which he was at home, and in which he made his reader at home. Moral issues were presented with sharp lucidity, and related to the divine will; and once so seen, could never again be seen otherwise. We who believe will ask no more. Belief is natural, for the world is so. It is enough to let it be seen so.

The Brink of Mystery, p. 46

9TH SUNDAY BEFORE EASTER

Theme of the Week: Christ the Teacher

==

The Images Given by Christ

The work of revelation, like the whole work of Christ, is the work of the mystical Christ, who embraces both Head and members. But, as in other aspects of his work, the action of the Head must be central and primary, it must contain in epitome all that the members fulfil and spread abroad. The primacy of the Head in revelation is seen in two things. First, the self-giving of the divine mind to man is fully actualized in the personal existence of Jesus Christ. Secondly, the communication to mankind in general of the human-divine mind of Jesus Christ is begun by Jesus Christ, who by that beginning lays down the lines of all further development.

Now the thought of Christ himself was expressed in certain dominant images. He spoke of the Kingdom of God, which is the image of God's enthroned majesty. In some sense, he said, the regal presence and power was planted on earth in his own presence and action: in some other sense its advent was still to be prayed for: in some sense men then alive should remain to witness its coming. Again, he spoke of the Son of Man, thereby proposing the image of the dominion of a true Adam, begotten in the similitude of God, and made God's regent over all the works of his hands. Such a dominion Christ claimed to exercise in some manner there and then: yet in another sense it was to be looked for thereafter, when the Son of Man should come with the clouds of heaven, seated at the right hand of Almightiness. He set forth the image of Israel, the human family of God, somehow mystically contained in the person of Jacob, its patriarch. He was himself Israel, and appointed twelve men to be his typical 'sons'. He applied to himself the prophecies of a redemptive suffering for mankind attributed to Israel by Isaiah and Jewish tradition. He displayed, in the action of the supper, the infinitely complex and fertile image of sacrifice and communion, of expiation and covenant.

These tremendous images, and others like them, are not the whole of Christ's teaching, but they set forth the supernatural mystery which is the heart of the teaching.

The Glass of Vision, pp. 41, 42

A Transformation of Images

The images are not through all ages absolutely invariable, and there is no historical study more significant than the study of their transformations. Such a transformation finds expression in the birth of Christianity; it is a visible rebirth of images.

The historian will see the transformation as gradual, prepared for within Judaism and outside it: but it precipitated itself in the thought and action of Jesus Christ.

There had arisen in Judaism the image of heroic and unmerited suffering for God's glory and the good of the brethren, especially in the figure of Joseph: and this image was tending to fuse with that of the blood-offering in atonement of sin. There was also the image of the Messiah, in whose enthronement the Kingdom of God would be manifested on earth. There were also images of the divine power and presence – God is in heaven, but his 'Name' is in the temple, his Wisdom or Word or Spirit is in the mind of the prophet, or, in some degree, wherever there is a mind alive with the divine law. There was an image of divine sonship, belonging primarily to the chosen people. In Christ's very existence all these images fused. Joseph the saint of sacrificial loving-kindness, the ritual Lamb of the atonement, David the viceroy of God, the word of God's presence and power, Israel the Son of God, Adam the new-created image of God: all these were reborn in one divine Saviour out of the sepulchre of Christ. All this he was by right and in fullness, all this the Christians were to be by grace and by participation.

If it is unreasonable to deny that the primary rebirth of images took place in the thought and action of Christ, it is equally unreasonable to suppose that it was so simply accomplished in him once and for all, as to require nothing but tranquil appropriation on the part of his disciples. The decisive act of transformation had taken place in him, but the whole furniture of images had to be touched and leavened by it, all had to be reborn with Christ. This process was one of great ferment and profound disturbance, and has much to do with the phenomena in which the primitive Church recognized the presence of the Holy Ghost.

A Rebirth of Images, pp. 14, 15

8TH SUNDAY BEFORE EASTER

Theme of the Week: Christ the Healer

Healing and Forgiveness

'Thy sins are forgiven thee,' said Jesus to the paralytic; for though he
pitied his paralysis, he grieved more for his sins. Those who stood by
exclaimed that God alone could forgive sin – which was indeed very
true, being of the nature of what our philosophical friends call a
tautology; for since sins are defined as offences against God, they are
certainly not forgiven unless God forgives them. Just as it would be no
good my forgiving one of my friends his abominable conduct to his wife;
only his wife's forgiveness could forgive it. Only God can forgive sins
and – this was what Christ's critics really meant – he does it invisibly
in the court of heaven, he does not speak forgiveness on earth through
any man's lips. They are wrong, says Jesus; and he heals the paralytic
before their eyes as the best evidence he can give for the claim that the
Son of Man has divine authority on earth for forgiving sins. Not God
only but man, not of course just any man, but the Son of Man, the
representative man, the proper man, the divine man, has this authority.
He is God's pardoner on earth.

Said or Sung, p. 61

The Slain and Living Christ

St Matthew's story of the paralytic abbreviates St Mark's account. St
Mark's fuller story reads like a burial-scene. The paralytic is helpless as
the dead, he is carried out like the dead by his four bearers; a hole is
opened for him, as for the dead, and he is lowered into it, as into his
grave. But, falling, he does not fall into clay, he falls before the feet of
the Son of God, who says to him first 'Thy sins are forgiven thee' and
then 'Arise and walk'. Jesus is by his own death the forgiveness of our
sins; he is the resurrection and the life through his own resurrection.
We are thrown into the life-giving sepulchre of Christ, we touch the
slain and living Christ, his body and his blood; our sins are forgiven us,
and we live by him; we arise to walk in all those good works that he has
prepared for us to walk in.

The Crown of the Year, p.56

Experimenting with Omnipotence

We must boldly say of Jesus that he inherited and used a stock of old-world ideas, many of which we have discarded. It was not this period-stuff that made his thinking divine. The divine thing was what he did with it.

Jesus inherited a picture of nature and of history in which God just does everything that is done. For the most part, he does it invisibly, and that is when we would say that natural law is taking its course. But sometimes God shows his hand and calls a human instrument, say a prophet, to enter into his intentions and to forward them . . .

The question of scientific explanations didn't arise because it was a practical, not a speculative, matter. It was a matter of discerning what in fact the divine will was set to do, and of making yourself its instrument. What God was doing had, no doubt, all sorts of scientific bearings; the inspired man did not need to know them. If Jesus could feel the force of vitality in the cripple and his capacity for faith, and the will of God moving to his deliverance, he could put himself into the hand of God and make the man well. To take an analogy: there are all sorts of scientific questions about the production of my voice and about the psychology of my attitude to my sermon, but you can cut all that out if you care to appreciate what I mean to say.

So the activity of Jesus is the direct appreciation of God's saving action, and the coming in on it. Or rather, he didn't have to come in on it, for he lived in it; that's where he was . . . The saving action of God sometimes impelled him to play a part in which nothing more happened than a prediction that a fever-patient would recover. Sometimes it impelled him to speak words of power arousing the faith that heals. Sometimes, I believe, the tide of the divine grace carried him beyond all boundaries known to us, and did wonderful things we cannot explain.

I will give you a formula: Jesus experimented with Omnipotence, and let it find its own limits. Maybe there were things that Divine Love would not do, because God loves the order of the world, as well as the happiness of men. But Jesus had nothing to fear. He would be shown as he went, he would know within himself, what it pleased Almighty Love to do.

The End of Man, pp. 74, 75, 76

7TH SUNDAY BEFORE EASTER

Theme of the Week: Christ the Friend of Sinners

==

The Sweetness of God

Let us suppose that we really want to know him. That is, of course, an enormous supposition. Really wanting to is far more than half the battle. For although the knowledge of God is not only the last, but also the sweetest, of things, it is the special malevolence of Satan to make it seem harsh and forbidding. We are in love with our own ideas, our own plans and habits, and though falling in with God is the only pure sort of happiness, we do not easily believe it, nor easily act upon it if we do.

The Brink of Mystery, p. 1

Searching Fingers

It has often seemed unreasonable that there should be more joy in heaven over one repentant sinner than over ninety-nine just men in need of no repentance, as though we gave most joy to the heart of God by often sinning and repenting often. But God has no joy in insincere repentances, and to repent sincerely is to repent, so far as we can make it, irrevocably. It is not for us to theorize repentance, but to repent; we at least are sinners, and we can give to the heart of God the joy he prizes so, for we can repent. Especially since the careful searching fingers are stretched from heaven to find the missing silver, and the love of God does not rest from seeking the lost sheep. How, in fact, was Jesus seen to be seeking the sinful publicans? He sat and ate with them. And he is seen to be seeking us, in that he has drawn us to share his table.

The Crown of the Year, p. 40

58

Growing and Flourishing

When a human judge acquits his prisoner, he simply gives sentence; he speaks the words, that is, and a clerk makes marks with ink in a book; the judge does no more. It is for his officers to show the prisoner out, and it is for the prisoner to walk away on his own feet. Do you imagine that God is like the judge? Or that God ever pronounces mere words which are but sound and breath? Men's acts are inexpressive, they have to explain them; men's words are inefficacious, they have to enact them. God's words and acts are not thus divided; his acts are self-revealing, the language of his heart, his words are self-fulfilling, the instruments of his will; 'Let there be light,' he says, and there is light. When God forgives, he does not simply pronounce or simply record a sentence; when God forgives, the well-spring of life turns from bitter to sweet, the acid of sin ceases to corrode, and living waters irrigate the soul. We stop shrivelling, we begin to grow.

Said or Sung, pp. 59, 60

Confession of Sin

I do not want to seem to be selling you a line of party goods. But perhaps you have the curiosity to know what people who confess before a Christian priest find in it. I reply simply that we find Christ in it. Christ makes himself most effectively present for different purposes in different ways. To feed us with his body, he gives us bread and wine. To inform us with his mind, he gives us the Scriptures. To confront our sins, and to speak our pardon, he uses a man of flesh and blood. You know that our Church offers you the opportunity, and does not constrain you to use it, unless you are so defeated in your life as to forsake the altar. Then it is a duty to seek the priest. Otherwise it is open to your free choice. And I wish I could convey to those who do not know by experience, how much happiness, and what life-giving power, resides in this sacrament.

A Celebration of Faith, p. 179

ASH WEDNESDAY

―

Do Not Delay

If there are any of you determined to live a more Christian life, there is one resolution you need to make which is, out of all proportion, more important than the rest. Resolve to pray, to receive the sacrament, to shun besetting sins, to do good works - all excellent resolutions; but more important than any of these is the resolution to repent. The more resolutions you make, the more you will break. But it does not matter how many you break, so long as you are resolute not to put off repentance when you break them, but to give yourself up to the mercy which will not despise a broken and a contrite heart. Converted or unconverted, it remains true of you that in you, that is, in your natural being, there dwells no good thing. Saints are not men who store goodness in themselves, they are just men who do not delay to repent, and whose repentances are honourable.

The Brink of Mystery, p. 17

LENT 1

Theme of the Week: Temptation

The First Temptation

There is nothing faulty, let alone sinful, about the immediate fixations
of desire. An appetite or instinct in our body clicks (as people say) with
an object or a circumstance in our environment. The clicking may be
positive (Give it me!) or negative (Change it! Take it away!). In either
case desire simply acts; wisdom comes hobbling after, and calls desire
to account. Shall we ask for a constitution of body and mind, in which
wisdom acts first and desire follows, taking her aim at the targets wisdom
has marked for her? We shall be asking if we do for something quite
different from human nature as it exists in this world. And since Jesus
had our earthly nature in perfection, there is no need to wonder how he
could be tempted. Hunger is innocent; a hungry man needs no bias to
the bad, no taint of inherited corruption, to covet a loaf before asking
whether he can have it. Christ felt the push of desire, he felt it struggle
with the wisdom called up to master it; and so he experienced temptation.
He did not yield to it. He hated hunger and longed for bread in the
wilderness of Judaea, he hated death and longed for escape in the Garden
of Gethsemane. He took his stand on both occasions with wisdom and
with God.

  If you or I, lightheaded with hunger, saw stones as the mockery of
loaves, it would still not result in a temptation, unless it were the trivial
one of cursing boulders for not being bread. Further than that we could
not go; for we should feel in ourselves no power of making bread out
of stone . . . Christ had the idea of an action he might perform, because
he knew himself to be equipped with the power or breath of the Father;
because, as John Baptist had said, 'God could raise up out of stones'
what stones have not in them to be; and because man may look to 'live
on any word breathed from the lips of God'.

  The sin of the heart lies in adopting the idea, not in conceiving it.
So in his first temptation Christ had simply to reject the suggestion that
he should profane entrusted power for the satisfaction of natural appetite.
He must keep it inviolate for the purpose assigned. The word of power
must be a word which, though relayed through the lips of the Son,
issued out of the Father's heart, in furtherance of his saving will.

The Triple Victory, pp. 41, 42, 44

61

The Second Temptation

According to St Matthew's story the issue turns on 'Son of God'. The baptism-voice has assured Jesus that the title is his. As a byname for Messiah it would express power and privilege. Should not Messiah, being 'Son of God', enjoy the free exercise of supernatural gifts? Might not he presume to approach God on a special footing, and do what would be presumption for other men, in putting divine Fatherhood to the test? Jesus's answer is to place himself firmly under the law of religion. To be the Son of God is to be perfect in obedience. Trust, not test, is the rule of faith. Divine Sonship is not an advantage held by the son of the householder over the household servants. It is filial devotion to the Father of the house. Since the Father's law is the Father's desire, the son will be above all forward to fulfil it. Christ takes to himself what was said to Israel: Thou shalt not tempt the Lord thy God.

So Christ sets out to learn his Sonship through patience and submission; what the Almighty Will does through him shows what he is. It is a terrible thing when the rigidity of a supposed orthodoxy robs Christians of a precious truth, the truth that Jesus lived like us the life of faith; when they imagine him to have had so flat a certainty, that 'If thou art the Son of God' could insinuate no real temptation. Who walks more by faith, or more by sight – the Jesus of the gospel, or his modern disciple? Jesus wrestled with a mystery far more baffling than any we are required to explore: he was called upon to be the Son of God in the world, when it was still unknown what it meant to be that. He had a brighter light in his own heart than we have in ours; for he had all candour and all good will, and he had the Holy Ghost. We, on the other hand, have far clearer waymarks on the road we are to tread; we have all the beacons he lighted and left us in his passage through the world.

The Triple Victory, pp. 59, 60

The Third Temptation

'All these things will I give thee . . .' If we take the bait to be the personal monopoly of all material power and glory, Jesus was incapable of being attracted by so monstrous a greed; he might as soon have been attracted by Satanism itself. But we are not obliged to take 'All these things will I give thee' in such a sense. 'All' can mean 'All or any of . . .' It's all for the asking. Jesus can have what he likes. Taken in this sense, the offer contains many items which cannot fail to attract a healthy mind. It is sheer morbidity to have no taste for freedom from hunger, thirst and cold; for any single charm or elegance of civilized life; for physical means to carry out good purposes, or to be the benefactor of others; for a position of influence to sway the counsels of mankind. Such things are good to have, could they be had on decent terms. Any of them may be refused for any of several reasons. They would distract us from the pursuit of more important aims; they would place us in a position of advantage over others which we prefer to forgo; they can only be had by employing detestable means. But from whatever motive they are refused, they are in themselves attractive to a healthy mind, and the refusal of them costs us a natural regret.

So Jesus is *tempted by* much of what Satan offers. Now no one is tempted by any object or any prospect who has no practicable means of attaining it. So, if there is any temptation, Christ must be *tempted by* what is offered him, and must think that there is some means of his getting it. His belief in the means need go no further than supposing that the person offering can make his offer good. But once the means or conditions for taking up the offer are made clear he rejects it; on those terms, no! 'Depart from me, Satan, for it is written, The Lord thy God shalt thou worship and him only serve.'

The Triple Victory, pp. 70, 71

LENT 2

====

Perversity

Perversity is both utterly inexplicable, and perfectly simple. It is inexplicable, because it is perverse; how can you rationalize sheer unreason? It is the one irreducible surd in the arithmetic of existence. Non-rational acts, like those of blind passion, can be explained by natural causes, as can the actions of beasts. Sensible decisions are explained from the reasonable grounds which motive them. Innocent mistakes may be explained by a mixture of the two: there are the reasonable grounds on which the mistaken man proceeds, and there is the interfering natural cause, the fatigue or the prepossession, leading him to misinterpret them. But nothing can explain wicked perversity; nothing can explain why reason, supplied with rational grounds, should wilfully falsify her own procedure in relation to them.

Perversity of choice is wilfully poor in the matter of reasons; we cut ourselves off from the grounds of explanation by being perverse. Perversity is simple with the simplicity of idiocy, or of the mind which refuses to think. And yet it is different from either; idiocy and the abdication of thought both leave the field open for the operation of natural causes, the overflows of passion or the automatisms of habit. Perverse choice is a real cause, creating the effect, but a cause which cuts itself off from reasonable grounds. It is both miserably simple and hideously effective.

Love Almighty and Ills Unlimited, pp. 140, 141

The Clash

We must put our confidence in *truth*. But that doesn't mean sitting back, and waiting for the truth to shine from above, as one might sit back and wait for the day to break. It means following with devoted obedience the truth *we have seen* as true, with an entire confidence in God, that he will correct, clear and redirect our vision, to the perception of a freer and a deeper truth. Go with the truth you have, and let it carry you into collision with the hard rocks of fact, and then you'll learn something.

What, then, did Jesus do? Did he sit still and wait for a spiritual revolution to occur? Or did he sit down and work out a new and speculative spiritual system, adapted to Roman imperial conditions? He did neither. He gave an absolute form to the religion which he and his people had; and then he threw it hard against the cruel facts. Israel was a nation, a kingdom. Very well, here am I, he said, risen up in the place of my ancestor David, to be your king. Never mind that it doesn't fit – that Caesar is on the throne, and Herod is his puppet. I have come to you so that, rallying round me, you may be the kingdom of God on earth; for the rest, we will put it into the hands of God to do what he will with the world and with us. The clash was inevitable: Jesus' kingdom collided with the priesthood of Caiaphas and the Empire of Caesar. He was crucified; and a new religion, liberated from racial bonds, sprang alive from the Easter sepulchre to conquer the world.

The End of Man, pp. 104, 105

Smiled into Smiling

When God forgives me, whatever he does he does not decide to let me alone, or to let it go at that. If he decided to let me alone I should drop out of existence; for in him we live and move and have our being. What would happen to me if the breathable atmosphere could decide to let me alone and were to stand back from me on every side, leaving me in a vacuum? But God is not like the atmosphere either, for though air sometimes becomes wind and wind hurricane, yet for the most part air just lies about and lets itself be breathed. Not so God; he is never inert, he is master, he is the sovereign will, he is always at work on me; if he ceased from creating me I should cease to exist; he does not let me be, he continues to sustain me. Nevertheless in so far as I profane and falsify my relation to the well-spring of my life, I begin to shrivel and perish, I am on the way that leads to everlasting death. If God forgives me while I continue to go to the devil, what shall it profit me? I go to the devil just the same. God forgives me, for he has no pleasure in the death of the wicked, but rather that he should turn from his wickedness and live. But whatever his good pleasure may be, I go on dying in my wickedness. God forgives me with the compassion of his eyes, but my back is turned to him. I have been told that he forgives me, but I will not turn and have the forgiveness, not though I feel the eyes on my back. God forgives me, for he takes my head between his hands and turns my face to his to make me smile at him. And though I struggle and hurt those hands - for they are human, though divine, human and scarred with nails - though I hurt them, they do not let go until he has smiled me into smiling; and that is the forgiveness of God.

Said or Sung, pp. 58, 59

Theme of the Week: Suffering

—

Natural Disasters

If I am challenged to say in one sentence why there are what men call natural disasters, I shall say this: it is because God makes the world make itself; or rather, since the world is not a single being, he makes the multitude of created forces make the world, in the process of making or being themselves. It is this principle of divine action that gives the world such endless vitality, such vital variety in every part. The price of it is, that the agents God employs in the basic levels of the structure will do what they will do, whether human convenience is served by it or not. Yet the creative persuasion has brought it about that there is a world, not a chaos, and that in this world there are men.

Would it have been possible for God to have made a world without a free-for-all of elemental forces at the bottom of it? I suppose not, but I do not know; and there is (I take it) only one Mind that does. Without answering any such question, I can be convinced that this actual self-making world of ours expresses the will of a Creator; and equally without answering it, I can thank God heartily for my existence.

A Science of God?, pp. 90, 91

Pain

Pain, and the remedial action which normally springs from it, are as vital as any functions of animal consciousness. Without them no living species above the most elementary would have the faintest chance of survival. Pleasure is a serviceable lure, fastening attention on the continued pursuit of a wholesome gratification. Yet we can conceive a creature capable of survival, which knew no positive pleasure, only the escape from pain. We cannot view as viable a creature knowing no pain but the lack of pleasure. It would perish in a thousand deaths.

Pain, then, is a natural institution which stands in no need of special justification. Pain, being the grip of a harm the creature has failed to shun, enforces the heed that was lacking, or evokes the effort that was unexerted. Even when the claws are not in us, the fear of pain, and the memory of encounters which sampled the ills we dread, will quicken the shunning of danger. Scalded cats and burnt children respect the hearth.

Love Almighty and Ills Unlimited, pp. 87, 88

Where C. S. Lewis Went Wrong

First, then, the moralism which is the strength of his thought runs into excess and overbalances it. When I say moralism I do not mean legalism, an ethic of rules rather than of love. Lewis was a Christian, he was no pharisee. But when he considered man in relation to God he viewed him too narrowly as a moral will, and that relation too narrowly as a moral relation. Man, to Lewis, is an immortal subject; pains are his moral remedies, salutary disciplines, willing sacrifices, playing their part in a drama of interchange between God and him. But this is not all the truth, nor perhaps half of it. Pain is the sting of death, the foretaste and ultimately the experience of sheer destruction. Pain cannot be related to the will of God as an evil wholly turned into a moral instrument. Pain is the bitter savour of that mortality out of which it is the unimaginable mercy of God to rescue us. When under suffering we see good men go to pieces we do not witness the failure of a moral discipline to take effect; we witness the advance of death where death comes by inches. By failing to keep so elementary a consideration sufficiently in the forefront of his scene, Lewis risks forfeiting the sympathy of a compassionate reader, for all the evidences of a compassionate heart he abundantly displays.

'*The Christian Apologist*', pp. 40, 41

Physical Creation Is Good

The problem of evil in any form only arises if we are inclined to believe in God, and in his goodness. For it is only then that we are moved to ask why, being good, he allows evils to multiply in his creation. Now we should not believe in the goodness of God, unless we were ready to acknowledge our existence as a blessed gift; and our existence is inseparable from its context, the world in which it is physically rooted. Believers must be glad to be, and to be in the world; they cannot, therefore, ask why God has done so ill as to make a world essentially of this kind. We could only wish the world had been made otherwise, if we could wish to be creatures of another sort. But we cannot; we want to be ourselves; better men, no doubt, and happier, but still men. We love our physical being: we do not want to be angels; and to be human is to be active in the world we know. Because we take the physical creation to be good, we are outraged by the presence of certain distressing features in it; but once they are proved inseparable from its general nature, there is no further question we can rationally ask. To regret the universe is either morbidity or affectation. The pressure of immediate sufferings may unhinge, indeed, the balance of judgement. Our derangement may be wholly pardonable, but it must not be allowed to pass for sanity.

Love Almighty and Ills Unlimited, pp. 60, 61

LENT 4

Theme of the Week: Transfiguration

===

Going out of Ourselves

It was by being outside himself – by being ecstatic in the literal sense of that word that Jesus brought the life of the Blessed Trinity into our world; for it is in ecstasy and in mutual indwelling that the marvellous life of the Godhead consists, God our Father goes out of himself to be all in his Son – this is the first ecstasy: and the Son goes out of himself to live by that very indwelling of the Father in him – that is the second ecstasy. There is a third ecstasy when there is a creation, and God comes out of himself to be all and everywhere and all things in his creatures. It is the fourth ecstasy, when the creatures of God go out of themselves to be in the God who indwells them. But this ecstasy the creatures of God scarcely achieve, until the Son of God takes on the form of a creature, and lives therein the ecstatic life: and when he died on the cross, he gave it to us for a legacy!

A Celebration of Faith, p. 103

Transforming Grace

What, then, is the attitude of the Christian to the sacramental life? Does he substitute form for spirit? Does he say: Let others seek for the free movement of the spirit in their heart and mind; I will receive the prescribed doses of sacramental grace? I hope not. There is a character sometimes held up to our admiration called the businesslike Catholic. I do not admire this man at all. What does he do? He goes and makes his confession (as indeed he ought), but having received absolution and done his little penance, he says, 'Thank you, everlasting mercy. That puts paid to that', and goes about his affairs; not seeing that he has flung away the best moment of all. Ought he not rather to say: 'The leak is mended. By the unspeakable mercy of God I am a sound part of the vessel of grace: the very stuff of me is body of Christ. O God, complete your mercy by a second mercy: save me from being an absurdity, a sacrilege; body of Christ without spirit and mind of Christ. Why did I come to be mended, except that I might hold the Holy Ghost? O God, where is love? Give it me! Where is your will? Show it me! But it is here already: in this care for you and for your concerns and wishes that stirs in me. Let me be this! let it fill my mind and person. Show me the prayers, the deeds, that follow from it!'

Sacraments are not inspiration, they do not move us like a play, they become very familiar, very plain. But in the sacraments we are body of Christ, and so we are fitted to receive inspiration. But we must seek inspiration, co-operate with inspiration, exercise and obey inspiration.

The Brink of Mystery, p. 73

The God of Beauty

There may be nothing that more readily moves me to the praise of my Creator than the contemplation of such a landscape. I worship the God of beauty. Human skill, I tell myself, is proud to have arranged a single pattern of aesthetic charm on a few feet of painted canvas; divine contrivance has set a whole landscape in everlasting rock, in rushing torrents and in springing trees. And in telling myself this I do not err. That adaptation of my eye to environment, and of environment to my eye, which produces aesthetic delight, is a masterpiece of God's skill. Not only has he created man, he has fitted him to his environment in a hundred subtle ways; among which not the least remarkable is this relation of things to our eye, giving aesthetic delight, and sometimes ecstasy.

Only I must beware of over-humanizing, or of taking the comparison between God and the painter too far. God is the Cause of the world's existence, and he has woven nature up from the bottom. That natural beauty which is such a charm in my eyes is, as it were, a divine afterthought; a sweet enjoyment for mankind in the look of a world whose existence serves quite other ends. Scenic beauty belongs to the sphere of man, and man was a late arrival. The masses of the mountains were not trimmed for human eyes; landscape is not a landscape-garden. God's goodness is not disappointed because not all scenes are equally lovely to us. God does not form ideal projects and regret to find them imperfectly realizable. He rejoices that rocks and trees, rivers and meadows, created on quite other principles, afford such feasts to human eyes.

A Science of God?, pp. 72, 73, 74

LENT 5

===

Captured by the Crucified

Everything that God does has an abyss of mystery in it, because it has God in it. But in the saving action of the incarnation God came all lengths to meet us, and dealt humanly with human creatures. If ever he made his ways plain, it was there. The variety of parables express the love that went into the redemption, or the blessings that flow from it. They are not needed to state the thing that was done.

What, then, did God do for his people's redemption? He came among them, bringing his Kingdom, and he let events take their human course. He set the divine life in human neighbourhood. Men discovered it in struggling with it and were captured by it in crucifying it. What could be simpler? And what more divine?

Saving Belief, p. 99

Our Eyes to His

We have met God, and we have God to meet. We have met him, and we have crucified him, we crucify him still. He suffers willingly, so long as our sin is mortified by his death. When we meet him, and see in his hands the impress of the force with which we have hammered the nails, we shall be in hell; but he will draw our eyes to his, and then we shall be in heaven. For we shall see them warm with welcome, alive with exultation, because his love has triumphed and his patience brought us to his feet. Then we shall share his joy, for under the eyes of Truth himself we shall not have the hypocrisy to grieve at what he is most happy to have done; and looking on his wounds again we shall find them terrible no more.

Lord I Believe, p. 68

73

Understanding the Cross

'To pay the price of sin.' And what is the price of sin? Not literally what it costs; say, what the prodigal paid the harlots. Christ did not pay for us to go on sinning. Then what price did he pay? What it costs to reconcile sinners with their Creator's will. And what does it cost? Surely not the serving of a sentence in some supernatural Dartmoor, or forty lashes of the best. It costs the abandonment of a false attitude, it costs a struggle against despair of virtue, a sacrifice of the pride which attaches us to the defence of our conduct, all the amends we can make to persons we have wronged – what else? The catalogue could be greatly lengthened. Such are the costs of our reconciliation, and such costs as these are not remitted to us, even by the sacrifice of Christ. We have all these things to do, only that Christ's initiative sets us in motion. He took us, and associated us with his divine life, even while we struggled against him. He has wrought all our repenting in us.

But still, I think, you are not satisfied, or you ought not to be; there is still something in the parable of penal debt paid which our story has not covered. No Christian can deny or forgo the claim that the blood-shedding of Jesus was the price of our forgiveness. And without the theory, however mysterious, of a debt to the bank of Justice, what are we to make of that? If there is no score to be cleared before God can forgive, surely God forgives us in any case, and before he sends Christ to achieve our reconciliation. What has Christ's death to do with the matter? Only, it would seem, to convince us that if we ever thought God did, or would, withhold forgiveness, we were wrong.

What are we to say to this? Let us begin by recalling who and what God is. God is almighty, and all his action in our regard affects our very existence. It cannot be supposed that God makes mere gestures towards his creatures. What could you mean by saying that he forgives? Surely not that he scratches an entry or pronounces words of indulgence. He who has the power and does not act is convicted of insincerity if he expresses the intention. Since God does not bear grudges, he has no need to set them aside; what, then, can his forgiveness be, but his ceasing to battle against our wills, and taking us into his fellowship? We, thinking by human analogy, will naturally distinguish God's forgiving us from his reconciling us to himself. The forgiveness is what would be, in a man, the attitude; the reconciling what would be, in a man, the consequent action. But God has no attitudes which are not actions; the two things are one. And so if Christ's blood is the price of reconciliation, so it is of forgiveness. And still there is no need for the theory of the Bank of Justice.

74

But even so, you will not be satisfied – at least I hope not, for you ought not to be satisfied with less than the whole truth. And you will still wish to say, will you not, that God has forgiven all men through Christ, even those whom he has not yet brought into reconciliation with his holy will. Yes; but his forgiving all men through Christ, even the yet unreconciled, is nothing so formal or so ineffective as the deletion of a ledger entry on account of payment received from a third party. God's act of universal forgiveness is the whole train of action he sets working through Christ, through the Spirit, through the Church, through all-embracing providence, towards the reconciliation of the unreconciled, whether in this world, or in a world to come. And of this great process Christ's blood was, once more, the cost.

Saving Belief, pp. 105, 106, 107

PALM SUNDAY

Theme of the Week: The Way of the Cross

———

Ordering Crosses

Crosses are never what we ordered, but always either greater than we ordered, smaller than we ordered, or other than we ordered – and it does not matter which; for God measures the love with which they are carried, and not the poundage of each particular weight.

Said or Sung, p. 25

An Unbreakable Fellowship

In view of the priests' rejection of him Christ was ready to conquer by dying. But he did not set out to be rejected – his work was not a ritual suicide. So we can ask, what did he set out to do in his mission to Israel?

. . . Shall we not say that he brought the divine life into the world of men, so that it overflowed upon them and drew them into union with itself? What else? He formed a fellowship with them which not death itself, not anyone's death, be it his or theirs, should break: for he was King in the everlasting Kingdom of God.

The Brink of Mystery, p. 112

MAUNDY THURSDAY

The Wine of Everlasting Joy

When the pious Jew, of Christ's time or after, had some happy occasion to mark, what did he do? His instinct was the same as ours – collect the people it concerns, have a drink in honour of the event. But it was the genius of those people to keep their feet on the ground, while their heads knocked against the stars. So the Jew had his drink with his cheerful friends, but in doing so he blessed it, or rather he blessed God. Blessed art thou O Lord, King of the Age, who hast created the fruit of the vine, and who hast made us happy in the birth of a son, or the betrothal of a daughter, or whatever it might be: so the formula ran. And then they drank the wine together, and tasted on their palates the very flavour of God's kindness.

So Jesus, at the supper with his disciples, said the grace in the common form, both for bread and for wine, and added the special point: 'Blessed art thou, our Father, King of the world, who hast created the fruit of the vine – drink this, all of you: this is my blood of the new fellowship.' They are to taste God's goodness on their palates; but it has a new and unthought-of flavour. God's goodness, which we taste in wine and in bread, in friendship and in every blessed thing, is the love that died in agony for our salvation. That is where the taste of it comes out; yet it is not a bitter taste; it is the wine of everlasting joy.

The Brink of Mystery, p. 67

GOOD FRIDAY

===

Mysteries of Grief

Before each mystery:
Our Father . . . but deliver us from evil. Amen.
With each mystery, ten times:
Blessed be Jesus Christ, very God and very Man,
Blessed be the holy name of Jesus.
O Saviour of the world, who by thy cross and precious blood hast
redeemed us,
Save us and help us, we humbly beseech thee, O Lord.
After each mystery, once:
Glory be to the Father . . . without end. Amen.

I
Sweat of Blood

Jesus in the garden prayed the prayer of nature, asking to live. Finding
it unprayable, he consented to die, and such a death. Then the Lord's
Prayer became the flesh and blood of the Lord who gave it. Abba,
Father, thy kingdom come, and so thy will, not mine, be done. Give
daily bread, give it from the altar of the cross. (He who prays has just
left the supper-table, and will presently be crucified to make good his
sacramental words.) Forgive trespasses, especially to these who sleep,
whose flesh is too weak to pray against entering into temptation; who
find deliverance in flight, and not in you when, sword in hand, Evil
appears.

II
The Lash

The love of God is never words, never sound and breath. His love is
Jesus, sent bodily among us, bodily living and dying, bodily risen. And
this embodied love of God meets a rejection and hatred which does not
stop at words either. No sooner has hatred pronounced the sentence
than hatred lays the lashes on. The lashes bring the hatred home and
hatred sharpens the sting of the lash. This, he knows with every stripe,
this is what they think of me. But love, however lashed, is not driven
out. The more it is defenceless, the more it shows itself almighty. He
has us at his mercy, having disarmed our rebel hands, now that all our
arrows are in his heart.

III
The Crown of Thorns

This is the jest against Jesus, his being what he is, King in the kingdom of God. The crown of his Kingdom is firm on his brows, for the thorns go in, and scorn drives them. Scorn forces upon its victim the hateful character it imputes; the scorn of the people, not the hand of the soldier, presses the crown on Jesus' head, identifying him with the mockery of what he is. So torture thrusts on him his joy and his glory, the sovereignty of God, to uphold through all suffering, all contempt. We that have put on the Lord Jesus have put on scorn, to glorify his crown in every place.

IV
The Cross

We shake it off, but Christ shoulders it, the cross, a burden not chosen but imposed and accepted. Among a world of men giving way where the load rubs them, Jesus takes the rub and carries the cross. It breaks his skin, it bites into his shoulder, but he carries it. What does he carry? He carries us all, for we who do not do our part in carrying drag on what he carries. What does he carry? He carries the dead weight of the world; he stands against the avalanche of cowardice and evasion, and when he is crushed to death under the weight, Father, he says, forgive them, for they know not what they do.

V
The Nails

The self-offering of the Son to his Father and his brethren is made absolute at last, and put beyond the possibility of recall. It began with acceptance, but it becomes necessity; our victim is nailed up alive immovable, incorporated with the dead wood. He is dragged through the breakdown of the body to the breaking of the mind, of which the last fragments and leavings are verses from the psalms: My God, my God, why hast thou forsaken me? – Father, into thy hands I commend my spirit.

Lord I Believe, pp. 92, 93

HOLY SATURDAY

Descent into Hades

It used to be dramatically taught that between the Friday afternoon when he died and the dawn of Sunday when he rose, Christ's soul or spirit was among the dead, and that being there he did not lose his time. He preached the gospel to the departed, and those who would have acknowledged him, had he lived in their days, acknowledged him there and then; for they were disembodied spirits, and in their action quick as thought. So Christ returned from the realms of death not solitary as he went, but leading Adam and Eve by the hand, a great train of their descendants following. He placed them in the Paradise of God, resumed his body, and visited his disciples. Christ's raid upon the world of ghosts was called 'the harrowing of hell'.

The mythical colouring of the scene will scarcely commend it to our belief, but the principles it embodies are rational enough. Those who died before Christ must be saved through Christ. Perhaps we would not wish to house them so discouragingly while they wait for Christ to come; but if we go so far as to place them already in heaven, we shall be struck by the surprising thought that it was a heaven without Christ, and therefore without the visible and incarnate presence of God. Can such a Christless state be heaven? Not if by heaven we mean that union with God, which is man's full beatitude. So we must call their happy limbo by some other name.

But if it could be conceived that a Christ dead and not yet risen might reconcile and receive those who, living before his time, had never known him, how far more readily may it be supposed that those who have died since without real opportunity to get a saving knowledge of him are reconciled by Christ in glory! The parable of sheep and goats shows Christ assembling all nations, and receiving into bliss those who, in succouring the wretched, had no knowledge that they were ministering to Christ.

Saving Belief, pp. 155, 156

EASTER DAY

———

A New Creation

Christian faith is a personal trust in Jesus Christ. But for what do we trust him? We do not trust him, as men have trusted human sages, to show them the way round a stable and enduring universe. We trust him to draw us into a new creation, and therein to renew and immortalize our being. I dare say you are sometimes tempted to think that it is mere adulation to deify Christ: the human life, the death, the teaching is the thing. But if you think so, you have not begun to grasp what the gospel is. The example and teaching of a sage is useless to us, unless the world will stand still; and unless the answer we seek is to be found in a present and fixed constitution of things. But if the key we want is the key to a new world beyond mortality, that key can only be found in the hand of him who has the making of it.

The shattering paradox of Christ's resurrection spliced the new creation into the old, and grafted eternity on time. The resurrection justified the goodness of God, not by explaining how every evil could be cured but by revealing a power and a love that promised total victory. The revelation was the life. Christ will do nothing to dissipate our anxieties or clear our doubts, unless we let him have his way with us, and draw us into the current of his immortal purpose. Humble your heart, confess your sin, accept renewal, embrace the whole of his will for you.

There was a splendid candlestick of gold in the temple at Jerusalem, carefully constructed to a pattern written in the book; I do not know of how many pieces it was made. The Romans came and took it away when they burnt the temple down. But St John had a vision: living candlesticks, the churches, flaming round the feet of Christ, and he, in the midst, the great candle of the Lord; his hand embraced the stars, his face shone like the sun at midday. 'Fear not,' cried he, 'I was dead, and behold, I am alive for evermore: I hold the keys of death and Hades.'

The Brink of Mystery, pp. 7, 8

81

EASTER WEEK

===

God's Supreme Skill

When we look at the circumstances of our day, and hope for the action of God's providence to get us through, it is natural we should wish him to act as we should act if we could; that is, by altering what we see before us, perhaps removing an obstacle, perhaps mending a bridge. But God's supreme skill lies not in manipulation on the existing level, but in drawing some new thing out of existent states of affairs. Even Christ began to pray in Gethsemane for the removal of the passion from his path. The divine will did not remove it, but brought the new life of resurrection out of it. When God removes evils in the human sort of way, it is commonly by the employment of human hands. His own divine way is to make unthought-of goods out of permitted evils, and to triumph by new creation.

Saving Belief, p. 57

Peace of the Risen Christ

We do not know what happened when Jesus Christ rose from the dead; that is God's secret. We do not know, that is, what happened to him, what change he underwent, what it was like for him to rise. We know some of the things that happened to his disciples, what he caused them to see, to touch and to hear. Through the signs of his presence which he bestowed, he made them understand at least this about himself: the whole Jesus who had lived with them before his passion was again alive, and with them again; nothing had been lost where everything had been glorified. We break the bread on the altar for the death of Christ, but presently we mingle wine and bread to figure the coming together again of flesh and blood in the wholeness of Christ's resurrection. And then we take to ourselves the words he spoke to the Twelve in the upper room: The peace of the Lord be always with you.

The Crown of the Year, p. 28

Living and Dying

Man's destiny consists of two parts: first we live and then we die. That is a platitude, but the next step isn't a platitude. In the eyes of God our dying is not simply negative, it is an immensely important and salutary thing; by living we become ourselves, by dying we become God's, if, that is, we know how to die; if we so die, that everything we have become in our living is handed back to the God who gave us life, for him to refashion and use according to his pleasure.

God desires that we should grow, live, expand, enrich our minds and our imaginations, become splendid creatures. He also desires that we should die, should be crucified on the cross of Christ Jesus, should surrender all we have and are to him; and he desires that we should die that death spiritually before we have to die it physically.

What then is the relation between living and dying? In a perfect Christian life, if we can talk of such a thing, the dying and the living would go on side by side from the start; life would be full, constantly enriched, and also constantly surrendered to God. But even in a life which has been Christian from the beginning, where there has been true surrender, true sacrifice from childhood onwards, there often comes a point of sudden change when the providence of God seems to say to a man, 'You have enriched yourself, developed and spread yourself enough. Hitherto your business has been to live and grow; henceforward your business shall be to serve my will, to use all that you have gathered, rather than to go on gathering more.' And when we look on men who have answered such a call, the saints who have given themselves to God and mankind without reserve, everything else looks cheap by comparison.

What after all are we to say about our dear, delightful, unconverted friends? We must say that so far as their lives are wholesome or truly human, they are splendid manifestations of the power to live; but that they have not yet learned to die, they have not made even the first step along that more difficult path which Jesus Christ opened up for us.

Said or Sung, pp. 13, 14

Christ Rising in Us

The death and resurrection of Christ draw near to us and touch us in the sacrament. The bread is broken – there Christ dies; we receive it as Christ alive – there is his resurrection. It is the typical expression of divine power to make something from nothing. God has made the world where no world was, and God makes life out of death. Such is the God with whom we have to do. We do not come to God for a little help, a little support to our own good intentions. We come to him for resurrection. God will not be asked for a little, he will be asked for all. We reckon ourselves dead, says St Paul, that we may ask God for a resurrection, not of ourselves, but of Christ in us.

The Crown of the Year, p. 29

Mary and Her Risen Son

Mary has seen Jesus crucified. The sword is in her heart, horror before her eyes; dawn wakes her to a blank of grief. They say, His tomb is empty – there are sentry angels – Magdalen has seen him – he is risen indeed, has shown himself to Simon; and on the heels of the message he stands himself among his friends. His mother lives again. She cannot keep him, but he is happy, and one world of love embraces them both. Only she wishes she still might live her life for him. Reflection tells her that she may, for on the cross he said to her 'Woman, behold thy son.' John took her home, and in serving him she will serve her Son. For, risen and glorified, Christ lives in his followers.

Lord I Believe, p. 94

EASTER 1

==

Confessing Ourselves as We Are

When Thomas said to his fellow-disciples, 'unless I see and touch, I shall not believe', what do you think it was? Was it a refusal, or a boast, or a confession? A refusal - I won't believe: or a boast - I'm too clever to believe: or a confession - I shan't be able to believe? He was a friend and disciple of Christ's, who had risked his life with him: how could he refuse to believe that God had raised him from the dead? or how boast of sceptical detachment, who had committed himself to a cause, body and soul? No, surely it was more like a confession: That's the sort of man I am; I shan't be able to believe, unless I believe my own hands, and eyes. If, when he said this, Thomas was telling the truth, he could hardly have done better: do you think he would have done better if he had lied? If he had pretended to believe, when he didn't? When we come to Christ in our prayer, shall we tell him a pack of lies? Shall we pretend all sorts of noble sentiments we do not have: pretend to believe in him as firmly as we believe our own existence, pretend to care for his holy will as warmly and constantly as we care for our own comforts and ambitions? Of course not; for whom could we hope to deceive? Not him: we could only deceive ourselves. No, we will confess ourselves as we are, and know that he will treat us on our level, and according to our need, as he did Thomas: reach hither thy finger, and feel my hands; reach hither thy hand, and put in in my side; go not in lack of faith but believe.

A Celebration of Faith, p. 79

The Resurrection Over Again

What shall we do? What else but the very thing Christ's disciples did from the first – early in the morning on the first day of the week reassemble the whole body of Christ, not a member lacking, when the sun has risen; and have the resurrection over again.

When we were children I daresay they were right to tell us we should not communicate often; but now we are children no longer, and how can we doubt that the basic Christian pattern applies to us? How indeed can our fellow Christians do without our support? The body of Christ needs its resurrection at least once in seven days. Seven, for Christ has hallowed the cycle of the week at a great cost. As the wheel of the days goes round, our Friday comes up red with his blood, and our Sunday bright with his resurrection.

What do you think St Peter or St Paul would have said if you had told them that you feared always to communicate, lest it should go stale on you? They would not have known what on earth you were talking about. It would have been all you could do to bring them to conceive the possibility of such emotional frivolity, such reckless individualism in a Christian man. What, is the body of Christ to lack a member because you are not feeling soulful? Don't you know that Christ wants you here, that he has died to give you what you here receive, that this is the weekly resurrection of the body of Christ?

Said or Sung, pp. 75, 76

86

The God of the Living

Christ's answer falls, of course, within the rules of the Jewish game. He has to prove immortal life from the books of Moses; and since those books do not teach it in so many words, he has to fix on a text in which the more enlightened eyes of Christ's own time can see the hope to be implied. He goes straight for what is absolutely central, the oracle at the burning bush. Moses asks the God revealed in fire to declare his very name; that is, to say by what form of description or idea he desires to dwell in the minds of his people. God gives a double answer: 'I am that I am'; and, 'I am the God of Abraham, of Isaac, and of Jacob.' Now the first answer relates God solely to himself. He is all that he wills to be, and wills to be all that he is, and nothing from outside him breaks the flawless ring of his light, the circle of eternal Godhead. The second answer nevertheless ties God to his creatures, and them to him: 'I am the God of Abraham, of Isaac and of Jacob.' Moses did not perceive how deep a truth lies here, but Jesus perceives it. The love of God for his saints attaches them to that self-grounded being which cannot fail. He is not the God of the dead, but of the living. For the love of God is not a sentiment, it is an almighty saving act; for him to love a person, and to let the person perish, that would be contradiction in God.

I said that the answer of Christ both gives the reason for immortal hope, and also states the substance of it. What then is the substance? It is relation to God. Do you want to know God, and to enjoy him everlastingly in all his endless power of creative renewal? Do you want to give God the desire of his own heart in enriching you to the limit of what you can take? If so, you have something to hope for in a life to come.

The Brink of Mystery, p. 75

87

EASTER 2

Themes of the Week: The Emmaus Road / The Good Shepherd

———

Christ with us

The Christ of resurrection did inspire and may inspire terror, for he is what we shall be on the other side of the fire, and we fear the fire. Yet we read that the fear of the disciples turned to familiarity and kindness, for whatever the risen Christ be in himself he came to meet them and returned into the place and into the forms of flesh and blood; he talked, he listened, he gave himself to be touched, he shared their food. For the man-in-God, the man utterly molten and fashioned in God's will, is not separated, not fenced off from us. How would that serve the loving will of which he is made the sensitive instrument? We fear the fire – yet all the fire will do will be to make us happy in living out the love of God; and Jesus, who needed no fire beyond the suffering of his passion, was moved by love to return among his disciples as the dear man they had known.

The End of Man, p. 9

One Mighty Doing

We believe in one God, one not only in the unity of his substance but in the unbroken wholeness of his action. All the work of God is one mighty doing from the beginning to the end, and can only be seen in its mind-convincing force when it is so taken. It is one God who calls being out of nothing, and Jesus from a virgin womb, and life from the dead; who revives our languid souls by penitence, and promises to sinful men redeemed the vision of his face, in Jesus Christ our Lord.

A Celebration of Faith, p. 62

88

Ties Beyond Death

Christ in glory is the heart of heaven, and it is difficult to see how those Christians who leave the life to come an open question can be Christians at all. If Christ is not now in glory, then this is a Christless world and God is a Christless God and we are Christless men.

Nothing is plainer in the faith of the New Testament than the ties attaching Christians to a living Christ. Because he is beyond the death we still have to face, our union with him is union with an achieved immortality. By dying, Christ not only made a supremely generous sacrifice, both overcoming enmity, and reconciling sinners to God; he also took the decisive step into that better state of being which lies beyond death. To grow up was good, to die was better; better, if only one could die right. Sinners die into death, but Christ, strong in the power of God, dies into better life. By communion with him, even in this present world, we plant a foot on the risen and spiritual state. Being incorporate with Christ, we are not only incorporate with the Son of God, we are incorporate with a man who has reached the goal of creaturely existence. Christ the infant was a less visible expression of divine sonship than Christ the man; and Christ the man of flesh and blood a less expression than Christ transfigured.

This annexing of an earthly fellowship to the heavenly state was begun when Christ, risen from death to glory, visited his surviving friends. Nothing like it ever has happened, or can happen – that the heart of heavenly being should visit earth, to leave on earthly senses the stamp of heavenly substance. No thoughtful Christian can allow the resurrection to be placed in one category with any other class of events, any more than he can allow God to be placed in one category with any class of beings.

Saving Belief, pp. 146, 147

Christ the Good Shepherd

Christ's parable of the shepherd escapes us not by being obscure, but by being so plain. The meaning is so familiar that we overlook it. What does he say? A man cares naturally for his own things. He does not have to make himself care. The shepherd who has bought the ground and fenced the fold and tended the lambs, whose own the sheep are to keep or to sell, cares for them. He would run some risk, rather than see them mauled; if he had only a heavy stick in his hand, he would beat off the wolf. Christ does not boast, as a man among men, that he loves mankind more than any other man, through a higher refinement of virtue. He says that he cares for us as no one else can, because we are his. We do not belong to any other man; we belong to him. His dying for us in this world is the natural effect of his unique care. It is the act of our Creator.

The Crown of the Year, p. 30

EASTER 3

===

One with the Bestower of All Life

Ought we to say that no alleged fact of gospel history should be accepted, unless it would pass the rules of probability which secular history would employ? Surely not. The methods of sifting evidence, or of reconstructing continuous event, which secular history employs are just as proper in the field of gospel history. But what of the criteria of probability? Secular history gathers its criteria from a flat-rate survey of humdrum humanity. But the man of discernment knows that whatever he is dealing with in Christ, it is not this. For anything we are to believe, there must, of course, be respectable evidence. But respectable evidence (in history) is seldom compulsive. We have still to decide whether the evidence suffices to prove such a thing as *that*. There is much evidence for Christ's resurrection; but, to judge from the general level of history and, indeed, of biology, would any evidence suffice to prove that the dead should rise? Ah, says the Christian, but to reduce the life, death and - yes - the resurrection of Jesus to the common level, is to beg the case. If Jesus is what we see in him, then he was personally one with the sole bestower of immortality; as John says in the person of Jesus, 'I am the Resurrection and the Life.' To make up your mind whether the evidence for his resurrection suffices, is just one part, but only one part, of making up your mind about the whole matter. To cut off the historical question of the resurrection, and examine it by itself in an aseptic historical laboratory, giving your verdict on it without reference to your general estimate of the truth about Christ, would be nothing but a piece of intellectual cheating. It would not even be good history. History must allow for differences of level. On the dead level of human probability, it was not likely that Shakespeare should write his sublimest works. But he was Shakespeare, and he wrote them.

Saving Belief, pp. 81, 82

The Transcendent Fills Every Finitude

The first capacity of the infinite is to fill every finitude. But it is a folly no less extreme to think that we bring God and his creatures together by attaching our temporal conditions to his existence. Is God to enrich his experience as he goes forward in developing the world-process? How can he, when there is no world-process nor any world-time? We cannot ask 'Where has God got to with the universe at the present moment?' We cannot rule a date-line across the galaxies and ask how things look to the Almighty on the first of June in the current year. Things are doubtless in their own temporal orders to him, because he sees them as they are. Their Creator is concerned to get each of them through the narrow gate of its own next moment, an aperture fixed and outlined for it by all the trains of event converging upon it. No such moment, no such gate confronts his own existence; unless indeed he is a mere constituent of the world himself, like the Apollo or Neptune of old mythology.

You can say if you like that every thought of God concerning a creature, and every act of God in a creature, has temporal form for God. What you scarcely can want to say is that all such acts or thoughts as he desires to make queue up for their turn of being his thought or his act. If you establish temporal dimension within each of his acts, you still cannot establish a temporal order among his acts. Consider, then, a mind or will capable of an infinity of acts without limitation of temporal order amongst them. How can you say that such a mind is geared to the temporal processes it rules? Whether we look at what we know of the world, or whether we look at what we must think of God, the conclusion is the same. The world is not such, that God could be said to live its history under the form of one time; God is not such, that his life can be confined within temporal dimensions. If he is to animate and visit his creatures, it must be out of his transcendence.

Faith and Speculation, pp. 165, 166

God Feels in Every Nerve of His World

We may say, then, that God's mind lives in all the world as my feeling 'soul' lives in my whole body or, to put it in antique terms, that God acts as the Soul of the World. It is better, by the way, to say *'acts* as the Soul of the World' than to say *'is* the Soul of World'. For if we say 'is', we seem to be confining God's action to the world he indwells or animates. When we say that the consciousness, or feeling-soul of any animal *is* the soul of that animal, we mean that its essential function is to animate that one body. We understand the 'soul' and its bodily house or instrument to have grown up together; or if either came first, it was the bodily system. Is there not some rudiment of an animal there, before consciousness dawns in it? All of this is implied in saying that the consciousness *is* the consciousness, or the soul, of the animal in question. And we cannot want to say any of this about God in his relation with the world he animates. To suggest that he is tied to the world-system in any such fashion is to make nonsense of our whole discovery of the divine. Our minds feel after God as Creator and cause of whatever system there is in the world; and to be this he must stand above it, and come before it. If God's thought thinks the world into being, his mind cannot essentially *be* the soul of that world. But we may say that in making it, he acts as its Soul, by feeling (or knowing, rather) along every nerve of the world-process he creates.

A Science of God?, pp. 85, 86

93

EASTER 4

Themes of the Week:
The Charge to Peter / The Way, the Truth and the Life

===

Our Tutor in Sonship

Christ does not preach a theory of the fatherhood of God applicable to the general face of things. He says you can get behind the face of things, and back to the heart of things, by living in sonship to God. So far (if you like a bit of jargon) Christ is an existentialist. The quality and the root of existence are uncovered by those who venture to live, and the truth is in the living. No one can do it for you; you have to do it for yourself.

A sort of existentialism – but not the solitary sort. Being a son to God, and having God for a father, is to tread, after all, a path that has been trodden; and Jesus, who knows what he is, proposes himself for a guide. 'None knoweth the Father save the Son, and he to whom the Son pleases to reveal him. Come unto me, all ye that labour and are heavy laden, and I will give you rest. Take my yoke upon you, and learn of me, for I am gentle and lowly of heart, and ye shall find rest for your souls. For my yoke is kindly and my burden light.'

When Jesus said this, he was quoting Jesus – there were so many who had had his name before him, and it is natural enough that he should have valued the inheritance. There was Jesus, the old don, the son of Sirach, whom we call Ecclesiasticus. And this is what he had put into his school prospectus: 'Draw near unto me, ye unlearned, and lodge in the house of instruction . . . Put your neck under the yoke, and let your mind receive learning: it is close at hand for you to find. See with your own eyes how I worked but a little, and found for myself much rest.'

I do not see how it can be doubted that the words of Jesus Christ are meant to echo the words of Jesus, son of Sirach. And so it is plain that Christ offers himself to us as a tutor.

So Jesus asks us to try his way; and who can consider it, without seeing that there is a depth of truth in it, the truth of life itself? Like a tutor, he asks us to be patient, in learning and in following his ways. But he is not a tutor in mere learning, he is a tutor in living; or rather, a tutor in sonship to God. And sonship to God is not passive obedience. The sonship of Christ is adult sonship – the Son shares his Father's mind, and has his Father for his friend.

The End of Man, pp. 108, 109, 110

94

The God Within

Who has not sometimes thought: If I could see Jesus Christ as he was on this earth; if I could talk with him, if I could have certainty from those divine lips, and read assurance in those steady eyes, then I should lay hold of God. So we think, but not so he teaches. He is in the Supper Room, desiring in that last opportunity to enlighten his disciples' minds and to assure their faith. But beyond a point he cannot. He cannot teach them as fully, he says, as the Holy Ghost will teach them hereafter. It is not so much the word of Jesus knocking at the mind's door that secures his admittance; it is the God within drawing the bolts with invisible fingers. When your pride, he says, when your self-sufficiency has been shattered by the experience of my death, the Spirit will secure the admittance of all the truth you need to know. And so it is: after half an hour's repentance before the cross of Christ, the Spirit shows us what years of study cannot discover, and what Christ present in the flesh might not avail to make us see.

The Crown of the Year, p. 32

Facing the Truth

It is hard to prepare for communion, because it is hard to face the truth.
But it is not at all complicated or puzzling. You have merely to accept
what you know God demands of you, and to renounce what you know
he forbids you, and to be sorry. Remember something to thank him for,
and someone to pray for, and you have made your preparation.

Then you will have to get there; and that will not happen by magic.
If you haven't waked before, you won't now. If you haven't a handy
friend to wake you, buy an alarm clock; there is no better use for money.
Do it tomorrow before you forget.

So you are in the chapel. Jesus said, 'Do this in remembrance of me,'
and 'Do' is the key, 'Do' not 'Dream'; do the actions and say the prayers
with all the heart you have. Open your book, say silently what the priest
says, and aloud what the people say. Cast an eye around and pray for
those you see. Offer with lips and hands and will the spiritual sacrifice.

Said or Sung, pp. 122, 123

Remaking Our Lives

The centre and the seal of revelation is Jesus Christ alone. The
significance of Genesis is that it contains the picture of an idea which
Christ proved by living it out. For it is not simply that Jesus saw the
handiwork of God in lilies, and his providence in the fall of a sparrow.
It is that he wagered his life on creative power. Who can raise the dead?
No one: in the literal sense, not God himself. The dead are not raised:
immortalized men are not galvanized corpses. What is called the
resurrection of the dead is a remaking of their life, in a stuff and in a
fashion which are known to God alone. If we are made, we can be
remade: he who created can create anew. Jesus Christ experimented
with creation when he threw himself and all the world's hopes into
nothingness, by the death of the cross.

A Celebration of Faith, p. 66

EASTER 5

(INCLUDING ROGATIONTIDE)

Theme of the Week: Going to the Father

==

The Birthpangs of Faith

When the disciples asked Christ to explain his departure and return, he did not explain the nature of these mysterious events, but he stated the principle or purpose of them. No birth, he says, without the pains of travail, but the birth of the child is well worth the pains. Unless we agonize at some time over the birth of faith, faith is not ours, it is not a personal possession, it is not the child of our own soul. Christ leaves his disciples so far and so long as is required for the pains of their travail. It is not an act of desertion on his part, but a merciful providence. Darkness and uncertainty, loneliness and spiritual effort are necessary to us, and, taken right, they are the growth of faith. They are as much the gifts of God as certainty and comfort. A little while, he says, and I will see you again, and your heart shall rejoice; your joy no man taketh from you.

The Crown of the Year, p. 31

If All Would Ask Sincerely . . .

There are things, difficult of obtaining, only in the sense that they cannot be carried away by a single pair of hands: peace, for example, and plenty. Nothing is more obviously to be had for the asking than peace, if all men will ask for it, without hypocrisy or reserve. But if one or two of us ask alone, however sincerely, how are we to get it? And plenty, too, plenty for the starving millions of the world which we ask today. That mankind, bending to the task, could feed all human mouths is evident, if all would apply to God for the will, and set aside wicked, selfish, or superfluous projects. But if one or two apply for the world's bread, how shall they carry it away from God's table, with their few hands? Yet we must pray for such things: since many pray already, and more may learn to pray; and there are many sound and natural desires in those who do not pray, for our prayers to reinforce.

The Brink of Mystery, p. 170

97

What Do We Wish For?

Christians say that Rogationtide prayers are superstitious. We should pray for spiritual blessings, and leave the great engine of the material creation to grind its inevitable consequences. Yet it is impossible not to pray for bread, when bread is short. The starving cannot be put off with spiritual consolations. Even if they will swallow them themselves, they will not be content to feed them to their children.

Prayer is always possible where wishing is possible, that is, genuine wishing . . .

When we pray, let wishing take its natural course. First of all, what do I want? Bread for the hungry. Then next, how do I wish, how do I hope it may be assured? My thoughts do not naturally run along Deuteronomic channels. I do not say, 'If only the divine hand would tip (as it were) the great waterpot of heaven our way, we should have first rain then bread.' I do not exclude from my thoughts a divine overruling of natural events – it seems that the physical world has in some respects a looser texture than we had supposed. I can still wish we may be spared floods and droughts. But my hopes and wishes turn more to the direction of human effort when I pray that God may give and preserve to our use the kindly fruits of the earth, so that we may enjoy them: there is still any amount of scope for the improvement of agriculture, and for the fertilization of arid territories, the world over. Why, it would be no fantastic feat to take the salt out of seawater, and pipe it all over the Sahara. It is not harder than flying to the moon; and it is certainly more serviceable. Meanwhile the Sahara is dry.

There is plenty of scope here for us to wish, and where we can wish, we can pray, can present our wishes to the Fatherly Omnipotence of God, knowing that without human wishes he is not pleased to move the mighty mass of men's affairs; but that equally our wishes are dangerous forces unless we submit them to him, and ask for his directive inspiration.

The End of Man, pp. 146, 147

ASCENSION DAY

Consumed in the Fire

We are told in an Old Testament tale how an angel of God having appeared to man disappeared again by going up in the flame from the altar. And in the same way Elijah, when he could no more be found, was believed to have gone up on the crests of flaming horses. The flame which carried Christ to heaven was the flame of his own sacrifice. Flame tends always upwards. All his life long Christ's love burnt towards the heart of heaven in a bright fire, until he was wholly consumed in it, and went up in that fire to God. The fire is kindled on our altars, here Christ ascends in fire; the fire is kindled in the Christian heart, and we ascend. He says to us, Lift up your hearts; and we reply, We lift them up unto the Lord.

The Crown of the Year, p. 34

Prayer in His Name

Christ is gone up. The mystical body extends, through Christ its head, to embrace the very life of God in God. Mary, lifting her hands among the disciples, prays in Jesus' words, in Jesus' mind. What she asks is what he asks, it is asked by God from God. The prayer of her love is a movement of the heart in the Blessed Trinity, it is the converse between the divine Persons, the asking and granting of filial desire. And so it is, when at one with Mary and all saints, we pray in Jesus' name.

Lord I Believe, p. 94

SUNDAY AFTER ASCENSION DAY

Theme of the Week: The Ascension of Christ

Christ on Our Side of the Ocean

It is a sort of childishness we all commit, unless we consciously correct it, to work with a two-decker scheme of heaven and earth. That is our great divide: on earth the familiar presences of flesh and blood, in heaven the mysterious Trinity, the holy angels, and the souls of Aunt Betty and Cousin David, departed from us in faith. When we think or imagine in such a form, what are we doing? We go as far as the first fence we meet, the barrier which closes our earthly perspective, and there we stop. Everything that lies beyond we lump together, as though there were no further fences dividing the territory. But the great divide – incomparably wider than any other, since its width is infinite – is the gulf which separates the Godhead from all and any created being. This is the Atlantic Ocean. The division between angels and men is only a parish boundary; that between men living and departed, a hedge between two fields. The Son of God is still on our side of the ocean, and in our parish, too, by his continued incarnation, or personal identity with the risen Jesus; only he is on the other side of the hedge from us. The company Christ has associated with himself is on both sides of the hedge; Christ is a man among men and we have fellowship with him by prayer and sacrament.

Saving Belief, pp. 130, 131

100

The Pattern of Daniel Remade

The writer of our Daniel was a great teacher - a great teacher indeed, for did not Jesus take him as his master? The preaching of Jesus turned on two phrases, 'Kingdom of God', and 'Son of Man'; and both of them derive from Daniel's pages. Though all earthly power is held by King Nebuchadnezzar or by King Darius, the Kingdom of God is sovereign and must prevail; though bestial tyranny - the lion, the bear, the leopard, and the bull - has trodden down the human form divine, the human form must triumph, the Son of Man shall reign; for God will not reign but through man, nor can man reign, save in God. So Jesus saw himself as that Son of Man, that true image of God, willing to face his destiny, and to be thrown to the lions, that his defeat might be his victory, that he might be brought up out of the pit and reign.

So Jesus lived out Daniel in the strange and unforeseen pattern of events, the unpredictable path by which his Father led him. And he, too, dreamed his dream. For, on the Wednesday before he suffered, sitting with his disciples on the Mount of Olives, he dreamt them their future in terms of his own struggle. They too, he said, like Daniel, like their master himself, would be condemned by tribunals, and rejected by their people: the Church would suffer a near annihilation, a corporate crucifixion, and yet the beasts would be dethroned, the Son of Man would reign, the dead would rise.

Such was the dream of Jesus - his dream for us, in which we have to live, and of which we have to find the very substance, by living it. He left his disciples his dream, when he went to suffer - the dream of how they should take his destiny, and live it out - but not content with that, he bound them to himself more closely still: he gave them himself to eat in bread, and drink in wine, that they might be his very self, each in his place, according to his calling. Daniel was a pattern for Jesus, a pattern he broke and remade in the living of it, but we have a better pattern, Jesus himself. What a calling we have, that we should live the person of redemptive love; should put ourselves in the hands of that will which is ever fashioning eternal glory out of mortal clay.

The Brink of Mystery, pp. 165, 166

Heaven Adopts Us

It is the obvious meaning of the ascension faith that Jesus is in some sense taken out of the world – not so that he might be made distant from us, but so that he might be freed from the limitations of physical being and new-minted in the image of the Glory of God. And so there are two worlds: our universe, the place of God's natural creatures; Christ's heaven, the place of God's glorified creatures. In either world God is everywhere present by his power and his grace; but more fully in that other world where the hearts of the redeemed offer no obstacles to his invisible action, and most fully in the glorious man, Jesus Christ, whom he has made personally one with his divine life. The mind of God speaks from his lips to the citizens of that country; they see the love of God in the kindness of his eyes.

There are two worlds, the old and the new creations of God; but if they are two, then how are they related to one another? Surely the answer of our faith is plain. Our world does not contain Christ's, but Christ's world embraces ours. Since Christ's world is not physical, it is no part of our universe: for our universe is nothing but an interaction of energies, a tissue of dynamic space, and what is not physical has no place in it. No lines of radiation which any telescope can follow will reach it, no curvature of light will show the pull of its influence. But our world is in Christ's heaven: for that is a world where spirit touches spirit. Those heavenly minds can know whatever minds are opened to them by God's will and permission: so we are present to Christ; and so he inflows upon us.

There is no way from here into heaven, while this life lasts; but all heaven adopts us. And so faith strikes boldly at the heart of heaven, and starts with the Christ who makes us his. To lift up our hearts, and put them with the Lord, is the beginning of our eucharistic action: and so it is of all Christian prayer. We have just to remember that we are in his world, known, yes and loved through and through, by the man in whom is the Godhead: and then to form our prayers as the extension of his thoughts.

The End of Man, pp. 37, 38

PENTECOST (WHIT SUNDAY)

———

Union about a Centre

The Holy Ghost is not a feeling, or a finite psychological force. He could not conceivably feature in a psychological explanation alongside other forces or components of the human mind. He is God, and God is the universal underlying Cause, not any created or particular cause. He does not inject anything into us, called either charity or inspiration. He continues the creation of our being out of its existing materials, and these are earthly enough. In particular, he creates that union of surface desire with profound intention, which psychology describes.

But the crucial point has still to be mentioned. The sanctifying action of the Holy Ghost is no mere name for any unification of the self which may have the sort of effect we have roughly depicted. The self may be pulled together by any object, interest or pursuit which is capable of drawing our deep instinctive urges in the direction of a conscious purpose. The action of the Holy Ghost unites us about a centre which lies outside ourselves, in the heart of God.

Saving Belief, pp. 121, 122

Uncorking the Bottle

On certain privileged nights in the University year you uncork yourselves. Like the wicked men in the psalm, you grin like dogs and run about the city, and grudge if you be not satisfied. But when you uncork the bottle, the spirit you expect to come out is anything but holy; not perhaps a spirit actually unclean, but a lawless, mocking spirit. Being sensible men, and realizing that one cannot live like this - that a little of this goes a long way - you charm the spirit back into the bottle . . . until the next Saturday night, or X's birthday party. And religion, you are quite clear, has to do with corking up, not with uncorking. Religion is indeed a useful piece of tinfoil to spread over the cork and give an airtight effect. Religion is not spirit; we know what spirit is - spirit is the devil and all.

But who is it that knocks on the bottom of the heart, who is it that says, Let me go free? No, we say, I won't have you, you are too dangerous. The mocking spirit of irresponsibility I can face; he hasn't the courage of his convictions, he lets himself be charmed back into the bottle. But who are you? And if I let you out, should I ever get you back? What would you do with me, where would you take me? It isn't on with me; I must retain control of my own life.

But, says the voice of the Spirit, I am you; I am the ground of your heart, the fountain of your true desire. I ask nothing of you but to be yourself.

Kneel down to pray, but do not rush into prayer. Rather clear away all the rubbish of superficial pleasure and equally superficial duty that lies on the surface of your mind, recognizing that it is there, but reminding yourself that it isn't really what you want. Be quiet, wait until your living will begins to move, and to long for the will of God. And once this *you* is alive by God's grace, what wonders it performs!

Said or Sung, pp. 103, 104, 105

Christ and the Holy Spirit

In the person of Christ, God acts through and as a man placed in the world beside me. But - yes - it is possible to conceive a still more intimate incursion of the divine. Perhaps the very ground of my being may be broken up, and the charity of God may spring in my heart. I see the amazing possibility; who is to deny that it lies within the power of God? Only, if this is possible, and actually available to religious faith, why is there, why ever was there any need for the intervention of Christ? The religion of the Spirit is all-sufficing. If the Creator can act on his creatures from the ground of the heart, and in the very springing-point of the will, why may not the Holy Ghost convert and inspire mankind, and so procure our salvation of his sole motion?

The answer to such a question must be sought for in the nature of our free will. God makes his creatures make themselves, and they must truly make themselves by their own principle of action. . . . The Holy Ghost is not a gift for us to use as we like, but a power using us at his good pleasure. Nevertheless our free will is his instrument, and he does not force it; he does not do with us anything that the set of our own purpose debars. His action is like the rising water of the tide, ready to fill every cranny that opens in the reef it engulfs, yet forcing no openings that are not offered. He does, in some sense, wait for the action of sinful creatures. It could not be otherwise. So, then if God wills to convert us, it cannot be from beneath the springing-point of our will. To say that we need conversion is to say that the channel is blocked. What, then, does he do? He forces upon us conditions in our creaturely environment which challenge our voluntary response, and, when the response is unworthy, shows it up for what it is. So Christ bears upon mankind, and his crucifixion shows us what we are. And it is by continued association with Christ that we are opened to the action of the Holy Ghost.

Saving Belief, pp. 124, 125

Making Us Alive

Is the Christian inspired? Yes, he is indeed . . . Only *how* does the Spirit of Christ shape our spirits? I am going, in answer, to give you a very dull word, a word which has no poetic colour or emotional aura – the word is, *attitude*. The Christian who seeks in prayer and sacrament the company of Christ, who puts himself into the acts and concerns of Christ, is drawn quite without consciousness, perhaps, into the attitudes of Christ. And Christ's attitude is a two-sided relationship: to his divine Father, and to his human brothers. The so-called Christian virtues are attitudes – Christ's attitudes passing over into us, to become ours. Attitudes, for example, of faith, of hope, of love . . .

The attitudes are the basic things, the immediate form of the divine life in us. But then, of course, they carry with them many particular illuminations. The mind governed by Christ's faith, Christ's hope, Christ's love, is the mind that sees straight, and so the convert cries with the blind man healed in the Gospel story: 'I was blind; and now I see!' Of course conversion to Christ brings spiritual perceptiveness: for it teaches us to look through the eyes of God!

Between getting one's spiritual eyes, and claiming oracular inspirations, the difference is wide. Oracular assurances are a *substitute* for intellectual sight, whereas what we are talking about is a clearing of intellectual sight. A good pair of spectacles is not a substitute for the use of one's eyes. When I have the advantage of spectacles, I do not say, 'My spectacles tell me so-and-so', but, 'I see such-and-such a state of affairs'. My spectacles do not inform me, they make my sense perfect, so that the visible world may inform me. The Christian mind quickened by faith, hope and love is simply capable of a greater perceptiveness. Heaven help the Christian whose prayers do not make him quicker of eye to appreciate another's need, and to hear the call of duty as it arises in every circumstance of life.

The End of Man, pp. 64, 65

TRINITY SUNDAY

Taken into the Trinity

The heart of being, the blessed Trinity above all worlds, is not a mystery by which the knowledge of Godhead is withheld from our inquiring minds. It is a pattern of life into which we ourselves, by an unspeakable mercy, are taken up. For Christ joins us with himself in the continual, practical, daily choice of his Father as our father. Why, he makes us part of himself, he calls us his members, his eyes and tongue, his hands and feet. He puts us where he is, in Sonship to his Father, and opens to us the inexhaustible and all-quickening fountain, the spirit of Sonship, the river of life, the Holy Ghost.

The End of Man, pp. 70, 71

Prayer in the Trinity

God above me, Father from whom my being descends, on whom my existence hangs, to whom I turn up my face, to whom I stretch out my hands:

God beside me, God in a man like me, Jesus Christ in the world with me, whose hand lays hold of me, presenting me, with yourself, to God:

God within me, soul of my soul, root of my will, inexhaustible fountain, Holy Ghost:

Threefold Love, one in yourself, unite your forces in me, come together in the citadel of my conquered heart.

You have loved me with an everlasting love. Teach me to care.

Lord I Believe, p. 23

Mind Is a Social Reality

Mind or will comes before all. But not solitary mind. It is a mere superstition to suppose that we know of such a thing as mind in isolation. Mind is a social reality. The characteristic act of mind is to discourse. Real discourse between persons comes first; the mimic dialogue of solitary thought is secondary; the thinker, by a fiction, represents the other in his own mind and talks to himself. But are there not hermits? There are. Yet even hermits talk to God; and even hermits were talked into talking, and loved into loving, by men, before ever they took to the wilderness of their solitude. Shall we say, then, that mentality, as we know it, is *plurifocal*? But now theology is the conviction that mind, infinite mind, is above and before all things. Are we then to say that the mind of Godhead is plurifocal too?

The grand rule of theology is this: nothing can be denied of God, which we see to be highest and best in creaturely existence. Now in us, personal relationship is as valuable as personality itself. Friendship, mutual discourse, common action – these things are as valuable as the power to think and to feel; without them, we might scarcely care whether we could think and feel, or not. How can we deny mutual relation in the Godhead? God is love; not only loving to ants like us, but related by relations of love on his own level.

The doctrine of the Trinity does not pretend to make God intelligible. It lays down certain requirements. It says that if God is to be God, the Godhead must be at once more perfectly one than any one of us, and allow also for a mutual love more outgoing than is found in any two of us.

Saving Belief, pp. 63, 64, 65, 66

Christ Reveals the Trinity

Consider, then, the picture of the Trinity in the human thought of Jesus, in the days of his flesh. He was himself one of the Trinity, so that one part of the picture was the picture of his own face, which his memory retained. For though I do not suppose he often looked at it, he had doubtless seen himself in water or in polished metal, and knew what manner of man he was: knew it, but did not much dwell upon it . . . If there was a light in his face, it was not through his studying of his face that it was illuminated, but through his study of another face. He knew his Father face to face; meeting those eyes, he forgot himself, and thence the light was kindled in his own. We read how, when he was face to face with his Father, and his own face shining, his Father's mind broke through to him in words: This is my beloved Son. And how, on another occasion, the voice was accompanied by a gust of power, an influx so real that vision gave it bodily form, a dove descending to settle in his heart.

Said or Sung, p. 116

Our Blessed Family

The disciples who were present at the Supper saw and heard Jesus Christ making Eucharist to the Father over the bread and the cup. They were witnesses of the intercourse between the eternal Son and his eternal Father. Mortal ears and eyes at that moment perceived the movement of speech and love which passes in the heart of the Godhead; human minds entered into that converse of the divine Persons which is the life and happiness of the blessed Trinity. Belief in the Trinity is not a distant speculation; the Trinity is that blessed family into which we are adopted. God has asked us into his house, he has spread his table before us, he has set out bread and wine. We are made one body with the Son of God, and in him converse with the eternal Father, through the indwelling of the Holy Ghost.

The Crown of the Year, p. 37

109

Becoming His Body

If a Jew blessed his food – that is, if he said grace for it – and added, before eating it, 'This is my body', his friends would not have been altogether surprised. They would have wondered, if anything, why he bothered to say it. It was his body, of course – his body to be; not actually his body, as any one could see; he would need to digest it first. But it was already consecrated to be his body, because he had said grace for it . . . Bread that is blessed is to be eaten, it is to be the eater's body. God has given it for that purpose.

When any pious Jew blesses his food – or when any of us blesses his – we may consecrate it to be our body, we cannot make it our body. Only God does that, the God, that is, of nature. Our creator, whose will gave us this bodily being, brings to pass by process of nature the transformation of bread into body, after we have eaten the bread. If any of us calls his food his body, he means his 'body-to-be,' anticipating the action of God, which will make it so. It is otherwise when Christ blesses bread, and declares it his body; for then the voice that speaks is the Word that made the world. It is the Creator who blesses, when Christ blesses bread. Creation, we remember, is itself a blessing. As God makes each thing, we read, he sees it to be good; he blesses his living creatures, that they may increase and multiply. We are what we are by the blessing of God; we join our wills with his when we bless him for making us what we are. At the Supper, the Eternal Son joins his will with the Eternal Father, blessing him who gives the bread to be his body. The blessing is creative and almighty. He says it is his body, and it is his body, by appointment of the will no creature can resist.

Said or Sung, pp. 124, 129

The sacraments are covenanted mercies; of uncovenanted mercies the number is infinite, and the scope unknown.

Saving Belief, p. 132

PENTECOST 2

===

The Overflowing of Christ's Faith

Whose faith is the Christian faith? I have said that it must be ours, but cannot be ours alone; it is the faith of the Church. But there is a deeper wisdom still. The Christian faith is the faith of Christ; not only the faith which believes in Christ, but the faith which Christ believes. St Paul cannot abate the claims of his apostleship, because he cannot deny the Christ who made him an Apostle; and Christ – he cannot deny his mission, because he too believes, believes in his own saving work; to deny it would be apostasy from the Father, and to die for his mission is the act of his faith. It is Christ's dying and rising faith which overflows, which runs as it were in the veins of all Christian men. Our communion is with Christ; and it is because Christ, by faith, lives in our fellow Christians, that our faith lives by communion with theirs, and theirs with ours.

Said or Sung, pp. 44, 45

The Great Bond

This sacrament is not a special part of our religion, it is just our religion, sacramentally enacted. It is whatever Christ is, and Christ is everything to Christian men. In particular, he is the supreme bond between us. Everyone of you communicating is bound to his neighbour by this, that the same Christ who lives in one, lives in the other. You care for your fellow Christian as you would care for Christ, and that in you which does the caring is also Christ. Christ in each cares for Christ in all when we communicate together. The same bond unites us with the saints in paradise, who make up by far the greater part of Christ's people, and with our departed friends who may not yet be in paradise, but for whom we care, and for whom we pray.

The Crown of the Year, p. 58

111

In the Silence

Try listening to silence. It is supposed to be silent in my house when I sit thinking of my sermon; but the silence is all rhythm, one rhythm overlaying another. The clock ticks on the shelf, a car faintly audible from a great distance purrs its way down under my window and off again into space and darkness. The poor tin clarinet of a little old man up the street is quavering a hymn tune. There is a background of pattering rain. There is the beating of my heart. I can capture and isolate one rhythm after another by selective attention.

Prayer is something like that – listening to silence; and directly you try, you find that silence is not silent at all. In the silence of the mind there are so many drums beating: noisy rhythms of self-conceit, of resentment, of lust, not to mention the busy intellect tapping out the various themes which amuse or which worry it; each of these rhythms competing for your attention, and setting you on to dance its peculiar tune. But you must push them aside and go deeper into the silence, until you can hear that rhythm which, though it may not be the loudest, is the firmest of all. You all in a certain sense know the voice of Christ. You could all of you repeat to me many of his sayings, or turn them up in the gospel. But it is another thing to listen to them until you feel the power and the life of them; until your heart dances in harmony with them, and your hands itch to act them out. That is the control that liberates, and the release that controls; that is the profoundest happiness.

Said or Sung, p. 184

PENTECOST 3

Themes of the Week:
The Life of the Baptized / The Church's Confidence in Christ

—

Only One Rock

The world's a boasting-match, a confidence-trick. Now confess, tell
yourself the truth without disguise – don't you envy with all the spleen
in your body those glorious beings who impose themselves on Oxford
society, those ladders between earth and heaven by which others hope
to climb? When I was a timid Balliol scholar of the third year I was
spoken to by a Trinity man. I could hardly believe my fortune. He
walked me round the garden and told me what was what; he took me
up to his room and gave me a glass of wine. I departed in a haze of
reflected glory. I inquired about him. He was a freshman.

All men are insecure. Each of us thinks it is his personal secret; but
believe me, we are all the same. St Paul elsewhere expresses the dilemma:
'Do I put it across on men, or do I put it across on God?' Of course he
knows that the language is improper; we cannot put anything across on
God. We obtain our security on that side by accepting divine love. Still,
there it is – which way are we heading? Imposing ourselves on the
world, or looking for a foundation in God?

Which do we do? Don't we do both, and hope to make the best of
both worlds? Alas, it does not work. For how are we to find the strength
of God? By getting beyond our powers and out of our depth. We shall
hardly know the miracle-working power of God, so long as we act well
within the scope of our own. St Paul pitted himself against impossibilities,
and never let himself off. And when he was weak, then, by the grace of
Christ, he found himself strong. The strength was not his, and the fact
gave him a deeper assurance. For every position of strength we build in
this world is sure to crumble. Only one rock will stand in the universal
whirlpool, and not be sucked down.

The Brink of Mystery, pp. 25, 26

Inspiration

Inspiration is, to Christians, a matter of faith. In the degree and manner in which they commonly receive it, it is not anything that could be publicly proved; and it is difficult to conceive what tests could be devised which would supply the evidence. God convinces us, somewhat as our friends convince us, not by evidence but by quality. The profound seriousness with which Christians in fact take their inspiration is seen in their acknowledgement of the Holy Ghost as a Person of Godhead.

'Holy Ghost' means 'divine life bestowed'. The Holy Ghost is *Deus ut donum*, God in the guise of a gift. Admittedly the language of gift is mere metaphor, and so equally is the language of indwelling. The creature has no lap into which such a gift could be thrown, and offers no habitation where such a guest could lodge. The language of gift is, if anything, the more dangerous, for a gift is commonly something which the recipient is welcome to use. And so far from our using the Holy Ghost, it is our privilege to be at his disposal, as the host is at the disposal of an honoured guest. Still, there is something to be said on the other side. A guest comes and goes and does his pleasure; a gift is given away, and so expresses less inadequately the sheer generosity of God. The metaphors do what metaphors are good for; they show the moral colour of the divine action. If we wish to define what happens, we must say that the activity of God's will lives in the action of ours, so that we say 'The more it is God, the more it is I; and the more it is I, the more it is God'.

Anyone who has genuinely prayed will know what these words mean.

Saving Belief, pp. 120, 121

Prayer and Dogma

Prayer and dogma are inseparable. They alone can explain each other. Either without the other is meaningless and dead. If he hears a dogma of faith discussed as a cool speculation, about which theories can be held and arguments propounded, the Christian cannot escape disquiet. 'What are these people doing?' he will ask. 'Do not they know what they are discussing? How can they make it an open question what the country is like, which they enter when they pray?'

Our creed shows us the truth of things, but when shall we attend to the truth it shows? The life of the world is a strong conspiracy not of silence only but of blindness concerning the side of things which faith reveals. We were born into the conspiracy and reared in it, it is our second nature, and the Christianity into which we are baptized makes little headway against it during the most part of our waking hours. But if we go into our room and shut the door, by main force stop the wheel of worldly care from turning in our head, and simply recollect; without either vision or love barely recall the creed, and re-describe a corner of our world in the light of it; then we have done something towards using and possessing a truth which Jesus died to tell, and rose to be.

Prayer is the active use or exercise of faith; and the creed defines the contours of that world on which faith trains her eyes. These statements are, or ought to be, platitudes. No dogma deserves its place unless it is prayable, and no Christian deserves his dogmas who does not pray them.

Lord I Believe, pp. 9, 10

PENTECOST 4

Themes of the Week:
The Freedom of the Sons of God
The Church's Mission to the Individual

—

A World of Opportunity

So far as men are concerned, it's true that in the end I have to make
my own life. I may open myself to mankind, but no friend, no teacher,
no human idol is to lead me. But God - no, God himself does not want
to keep me in infantile leading-strings, either. It will be enough if I
open myself to admire what deserves admiration, to love what is worthy
of love, and to learn what most repays attention. To think that a
preoccupation with my own clever pursuits, or the scoring of my own
little successes, should ever close my eyes to the work God works in the
whole fabric of this world, and in my neighbour, and in myself! The
more I see of the wisdom of his work, and of the depth of his love, the
more, not less, will be the calls on my powers of origination or
contrivance. In a vacuum of emptiness our manly freedom would go for
nothing. God is the very world of opportunity to his saints. He so
enriches their environment by his manifold presence, they have more
than enough to do, now and to all eternity.

The End of Man, pp. 46, 47

One Individual, who Killed Himself

Philip and I had been close acquaintances for three years. Why, we had even lodged together for one of them. We were naturally attracted to one another, we had common studies, common hobbies; I should say as a Christian that God had given him to me for a friend. Yet I had watched him drift into a useless way of life. Couldn't I have helped him at all? Well, perhaps I wasn't a very strong character; and it's no use talking about that. But I can see - and this, surely, is deplorable - that religion got in the way. Philip was very nice, and he respected my faith, though he scarcely shared it. He regarded me as a pious innocent, whose ears should not be vexed by hearing what would grieve them; and I acquiesced in this provision for my mental comfort: with the result that whatever it was that was eating out his heart, I wasn't going to know. I thought that if I was to help him, I ought to come the Christian over him, and convert him to a lively faith: but in that mutually sealed-off relationship in which we stood, nothing was more unlikely than my being able to help him in such a way.

I suppose (I cannot well remember) that I prayed for the man: but it is not much use in such a case praying for people if your prayer consists in telling God to make them good Christians. We should do better, if we were telling God all the good and delightful qualities he has put into our friend, and were thanking him for them with all sincerity. When you have blessed God for your friend, you can go on to pray for his blessing by God. This is the sort of prayer that breaks down barriers: it is the way to accept our friends as God's good handiwork, and to delight in them. And then, when we talk with them, we mustn't be constantly forcing their thoughts into the mould of our own moral orthodoxy: we've got to take them as they are, to go with them in working out their own way. And that need never mean that we help them in going to the devil. There is good somewhere in every heart, with which we can sympathize: it may not be a good tailored to the pattern of our ideas.

The Brink of Mystery, pp. 58, 59

117

Freedom to Respond to Reality

If God is the creative spring of all being, and the inexhaustible fountain
of all newness - that is, if God is God - one is no more enslaved by
dependence on him than one is enslaved by the habit of breathing. If,
on the other hand, God is an idol of the human mind, one is enslaved
by obsession with so tyrannical an idea. What is a *free-thinker*? Not, I
suppose, a man who maintains freedom of mental manoeuvre by refusing
submission to true facts. Freedom can only be freedom to embrace and
explore the world; not even the humanist can create his universe: he
must respond to realities according to the demands they make on him;
and it cannot surprise him that, in the eyes of a believer, the supreme
freedom should be freedom to know God and to respond to him.

Is the acceptance of God as my God a cramping acceptance? Well,
is the acceptance of my neighbour as my neighbour a cramping
acceptance? X married a wife, kind and clever and better than he
deserved. X deserts her in the midst of her second pregnancy. His wife
cramps him; he wants to be off with a fascinating blonde. She cramps
him, for she puts a limitation on his freedom of action. But she exists,
and so do her children. She loves him (blast her!) and the children need
a father. Besides, he gave his word. Reality is a nuisance to those who
want to make it up as they go along. But then, while every wife is
actually limiting - she is a finite good; there are charms she doesn't
possess, and another will - God does not limit us by being limited; he
only limits us by being true.

Saving Belief, pp. 33, 34

PENTECOST 5

====

The Attraction of the Heart

(The reference is to the Book of Ruth)

What Ruth did was unnecessary but there is no getting over the fact
that this is exactly why we like her. The more casual, quixotic unnecessary
self-devotion is, the more it takes our affections. There is something
random, indeed, about all personal devotion . . . We *fall for* someone,
as the saying goes; and often it seems that it might just as well have
been for someone else. When did Ruth take the plunge? There in the
middle of the path, I fancy, she suddenly knew she wouldn't go back.
But if her choice was sudden, it wasn't light or fickle. This girl, if she
gave herself, she gave herself, 'Whither thou goest I will go and where
thou lodgest I will lodge, thy people shall be my people and thy God
my God. The Lord slay me and worse, if aught but death part me and
thee.'

Well, but can sheer choice, the attraction of the heart into irrevocable
commitment, be the best thing in the world, the key to our paradise?
What is the use of disputing about it? We know it is so, with the only
sort of knowledge available on such a matter.

If there is something always irrational and outside the reckoning about
human self-devotion, what shall we say of the act by which the Divine
Son descends from the mountains of his glory to meet us on the roads
of our migration, making our concern and our life and our flesh and
blood his own? His loving-kindness is the Ruth that goes, that goes –
where? To the very place where Ruth brought Naomi on her way – for,
it says, they came to Bethlehem in the beginning of barley-harvest.
Ruth, devoting herself, making herself over, came to Bethlehem, not
knowing what part was assigned to her there in the providence of God.
She came to Bethlehem, and was received by marriage into the family
from whom Jesse and David, and so ultimately Jesus Christ according
to the flesh, was born: St Matthew names her among Christ's ancestors.
She came to Bethlehem, to take a preparatory and unknowing part in
that act of devotion by which the living Love came down and made
himself ours everlastingly in flesh and blood that he might make us his.

The End of Man, pp. 90, 91, 92, 93

Whom Should We Help?

Some responsibilities for things and persons are defined and enforced by law. But the good man accepts many of them on their merits, and is his own judge with regard to them. Parents, for example, seldom need the magistrate to teach them their responsibility for their children. The next step is to extend the notion beyond the extremest range of law. The legislator, we will say, is a rough schoolmaster to train us in a few typical responsibilities, and to enforce a few vital ones. But the good-hearted man comes to acknowledge responsibility for everything human which falls in his path. He is his brother's keeper; his neighbour is whoever meets him; the responsibilities that may arise for him are defined neither by law nor by custom, but by the pull of facts.

But how will you hold Dives responsible for Lazarus on his doorstep, when the doorstep is the world, and Lazarus is every ascertainable distress? We cannot be held responsible for mankind, nor for all the men who come our way; but only for seeing them, and for praying to be given discretion, whom we should help, and whom let be . . .

To do what is right often means to make a succession of serious or virtuous decisions in face of the morally relevant facts. And such decision can be as inventive as any. We have to make it up as we go along – we have to; the moral facts put us on our mettle, and forbid our invention to flag.

The Freedom of the Will, pp. 276, 277

The Wish of the Legislator's Heart

We have to see Jesus as a teacher who used the classroom instruments of his time. The Old Testament and especially the writings of Moses provided the textbook. Here were the laws which the God of Israel was deemed to have given, to discipline a fierce and wayward tribe. What was one to do with them? The Pharisaic doctors multiplied ingenious comment, partly to soften, to argue away what was barbarous or obsolete, partly to fit the statute by minute regulation to every circumstance of contemporary life. All this comment Jesus swept away. He said in effect, Take the law as it stands, and ask yourself not, What did God permit? (he may have been grieved to permit it) nor, How much did God exact? (it may have been all that could be enforced) but, What did the Lord who gave each law desire from willing servants, not to say loyal sons? He commands you to love your neighbour; does he desire you to hate your enemy? He directs judges to award exact retribution if a suit is brought into court. Does he desire that suits should be brought, rather than injuries forgiven? He forbids adultery; what lusts does he approve? Honour the sabbath by a holy rest, love your neighbour as yourself. But see, it is sabbath, you are a healer, your neighbour is in pain; what does the God who gave these two commands desire that you should do?

I leave it for you to judge whether this teaching is legalist or anti-legalist. Christ said he was increasing the stringency of written law, by referring us to the very wish of the legislator's heart. If that is legalism, it is also something more. It leaves us the written law for a ready guide, but it throws us on a knowledge of the heart of God . . . I do not know how I am to trust my own heart to echo the divine, without that union with God in Christ, which our religion promises to the believing penitent.

Saving Belief, pp. 117, 118

PENTECOST 6

═══

Enjoyment

The best way of thanking God is to taste his goodness with all our palate. It is no use making speeches of thanks to a musician, if you are bored by his performance. You may deceive him, indeed, if you are a clever hypocrite, and can act the attention you can't be bothered to bestow. But God reads our hearts, and he knows whether we taste his kindness, or not. Enjoyment is the sincerest thanks.

The Brink of Mystery, pp. 67, 68

A New Song

A pair of nightingales in Exeter College garden were singing their hearts out. His own heart turned over in his breast. The performance, indeed, was not new; we have heard nightingales before; and nightingales have been singing the same song since long before mankind got the wit to enjoy them. Yet, though there is nothing fresh for them to sing, they sing freshly, their singing is their life, they are not putting on a stale record. And it is a stale ear in my human head that cannot feel the freshness, or yield to the magic of it. 'Sing unto the Lord a new song', says the old Psalmist, for God's most strange love is insulted by a stale adoration. And yet the newness will not be in the song, since there is nothing new to sing; but in the singers, to whom God may perpetually grant a newness of heart, in voicing his praise. Our tired imaginations see eternal sameness in the chanting of heavenly spirits; and yet, says St John, they sing a new song in honour of a wonder which can never grow old. For as God in the cradle is a wonder on earth, which angels celebrate, and shepherds adore; so man on the celestial throne is a marvel in heaven, which those heavenly eyes can never cease to drink in with amazement.

The Brink of Mystery, p. 107

122

Half Wishes

I say that our wishes, un-translated into prayer, are dangerous things. Dangerous things? There is little danger, heaven knows, in those half-wishes, and less than half-wishes, for virtuous objects, which we dutifully serve up in our prayers. What good are they to God, or to us? May God help us to find, and to acknowledge, to liberate and to submit unto his will the fountains of sincere desire which are the life-blood of our mind. This is the evil of Christian hypocrisy: while we are dramatizing ourselves into correct but ineffectual attitudes before God, we cut ourselves off from the springs of genuine will. It was never said of a true saint, you couldn't see what made him tick.

The End of Man, p. 147

Consideration to All, Devotion to Some

I prefer to talk of considerateness to all, rather than politeness. For politeness is really no more than a set of customs which express consideration for others on the whole, and in ordinary circumstances.

But genuine considerateness towards others is the whole religion of some serious men, and half the religion of a great many. Considerateness to all, devotion to some: we cannot be devoted to all, there is not enough of us to cover such an undertaking. We have to reflect both the universality and the intensity of God's love. But we have to be content to let the universality and the intensity go apart. The intensity of God's love we must pray to reflect in our devotion for those whom God has specially given us to be ours – or rather, perhaps, those to whom God has specially given us, to be theirs. But the universality of God's love we must endeavour to reflect in considerateness for all with whom we have to do. The universality and the intensity of concern for others must go apart in us. They are one thing in God, for he loves every one of his creatures with an entire and inexhaustible love. He has an infinite heart, and we have not.

Said or Sung, pp. 165, 166

PENTECOST 7

Theme of the Week: The More Excellent Way

——

The Two Circles

The occasions for kindness ring us round in two circles. The inner circle
is made up of our ordinary environment. How do you view the people
among whom you move? Are you going to cultivate the successful and
neglect the less attractive and keep out of the way of the queer? Are you
ever going to ask, who needs friendship most? Of course there is a special
place for our most congenial friends; it is another thing, if we shutter
our minds against others, or close our doors.

So much for the inner circle of kindness, which touches us all the
time; so surely it concerns us most. But then there is the outer circle,
more distant, hungry and dark – the needs of those less privileged than
we are.

The Brink of Mystery, p. 55

Love Is Natural

For my part I would rather say that love is entirely natural, being nothing more nor less than honesty of heart. For the heart has its honesty, just as the mind has. It is honesty in the mind to acknowledge truth of fact without distortion; it is honesty in the heart to give to every being the response it calls for. Are not these simply the attitudes that make a man? An animal feels certain salient features of its environment and is capable of affection for a few of its own sort. A man, through largeness of mind, is open to the universe, and capable of caring for whatever he can understand. If only it were as easy to enlarge the heart, as it is to stretch the intellect! Honesty of mind can be commonly achieved by effort or attention; goodness of heart is not similarly at our command. I can make myself acknowledge the truth, however unwelcome; I cannot similarly make myself love what calls for love; for love goes by liking.

It is not surprising, then, that we feel more moved to pray for charity, than to pray for mental integrity. We naturally want to ask God for what we cannot get ourselves. And that may be one reason why charity has been thought a supernatural grace, the gift of God. We have little power to make ourselves love, where we do not; but it remains perfectly natural in us to love, where we do.

Where we do not love, it is right that we should endeavour to act as though we loved; but how poor a second best that is! One experience of deep, genuine, and unforced appreciation, one simple devotion to any fellow-creature, is a clue to the worth of God's whole handiwork, and an exploration of the Maker's glory. What is the thing that God has truly made? It is the thing that the eye of love perceives. Where love moves us, God moves us. The heart is the organ through which our Creator's goodness is acknowledged and echoed in us.

The Brink of Mystery, pp. 28, 29

At the Service of Reverence and Love

When it is said that theological belief is morally irrelevant, because after all, God or no God, we have to explore the facts to decide a policy of action, and in deciding, trust our aspiration, we make answer that moral policies are at the service of reverence and love, and that as soon as we consider what we reverence, what we love, the practical bearing of theology appears. For it is no trifling difference, whether we value our neighbour simply for what he is, or for the relation in which he stands to the will of God; a will establishing his creation, and intending his perfection. Those that are so minded reverence not a single, but a double object, God in their neighbour, and their neighbour in God. The divine is not far removed from them, but touches them as nearly as physical things touch them. For the physical is known to us by the way it conditions our physical motion; and the divine will, which is God himself, is known to us in limiting or evoking our dutiful action, through all the persons with whom we have to do.

The Freedom of the Will, p. 309

Which Invitation?

An overmastering sense of human ills can be taken as the world's invitation to deny her Maker, or it may be taken as God's invitation to succour his world. Which is it to be? Those who take the practical alternative become more closely and more widely acquainted with misery than the onlookers; but they feel the grain of existence, and the movement of the purposes of God. They do not argue, they love; and what is loved is always known as good. The more we love, the more we feel the evils besetting or corrupting the object of our love. But the more we feel the force of the besetting harms, the more certain we are of the value residing in what they attack; and in resisting them are identified with the action of God, whose mercy is over all flesh.

Love Almighty and Ills Unlimited, p. 188

PENTECOST 8

Theme of the Week: The Fruit of the Spirit

==

Turn Your Face

Do not suppose that you can store grace within yourself, and carry on. It cannot be done. Grace flows like sunlight from God to us, and can no more be stored than sunlight can be stored. You must turn your face to the rays.

The Brink of Mystery, p. 26

The Holy Ghost as Our Very Soul

The gift of the Holy Ghost closes the last gap between the life of God and ours. Our Father and Maker certainly underlies and sustains our existence at every point, and yet an impenetrable veil hides him from us. The veil has no thickness, and yet we cannot see through it; his life is his, and our life is ours. The Son of God steps through the veil, clothed in our nature; he becomes one of us, he takes his place beside us in this very sacrament. Nevertheless the more Jesus Christ is revealed as a man, the more distinct he is from us, for each of us is another man. But the Holy Ghost is given by the Father and the Son to be our very soul. When we allow the love of God to move in us, we can no longer distinguish ours and his; he becomes us, he lives us. It is the firstfruits of the Spirit, the beginning of our being made divine.

The Crown of the Year, p. 41

The Indispensable near Impossibility

It is nearly impossible to pray, but the overcoming of that impossibility, that is just what prayer is. If you could pray when you set yourself to pray, then perhaps you would not need to pray. For perhaps it is right to say that the blessed saints in heaven do not pray, they simply look upon the face of God and rejoice in the overflow of everlasting light. But you have got to pray – you have got to pray yourself out of prayerlessness. Do you care about the happiness of your friends? Very little. Do you care about their salvation? Not at all. Then must your prayers for them be insincere? Yes, they will be insincere while they are yours, for you are insincere, as insincere in your worldliness as you are insincere in your charity and faith. Nevertheless, pray in your insincerity, until your prayers cease to be yours alone, until the sun of God's charity has warmed you into life, and turned your heart of stone to a heart of flesh. You do not believe in God. No, but neither do you disbelieve. Your disbelief and your belief are insincere alike. Pray your insincere prayer until he who is sincerity and truth itself overcomes you, until his rays prise open your eyes, and you see that most blessed sight, a living love, a living will, a flame to cauterize your meanness and your frivolity, a light to sweeten every stale corner of your thought, a life better than your own in which to live. Go out and walk in that light – but the darkness will have you again, but you must pray again, be continually reborn. How dare you start the day in darkness, and not have prayed, or go in darkness and without prayer to rest?

The End of Man, pp. 28, 29

The Springs of Our Action

What is the grace of Christ? It is that Christ penetrates us, and that this penetration has real effects. It is our prejudice to think that all persons are separate units, and that we communicate only by signalling to one another across physical spaces by physical signs, whether gestures or words. Such is our prejudice. It is called common sense, but it simply is not true. In the word of the spirit our prayers invade and enliven one another; and what are our prayers? They are our souls in action. The saints support and carry us; their life is the life of the Church. But the saints themselves, and we, are supported and enlivened by Jesus Christ. For he, being God, is also man; he crosses from the divine side to ours, to share with us as we share with one another; to be the heart in that community of spiritual creatures which serves the Father Almighty.

So grace is Jesus Christ entering us, Jesus Christ under the skin, the sacrifice of Jesus and the resurrection of Jesus spreading and fulfilling themselves in us. As the well-known prayer expresses it, 'Soul of Christ hallow me, Body of Christ save me, Blood of Christ enflame me, Passion of Christ strengthen me.'

The effects of grace are put down by unbelievers to suggestion, individual or corporate. Nothing comes in from outside, they say; it is all something into which we think ourselves. In a sense, Christians do not disagree; nothing comes in from outside; it is just us, thinking ourselves into our best nature. It is just us; but what are we? That is the point, what are we? According to the unbelieving philosophy, we are complex single beings; but according to faith, we are complex double beings. At a level deeper than that which any science studies, Christ feeds with himself the springs of our action. Nothing comes in from outside; when we act from the resources of divine grace, all the action and all the thought is in us; but it is Christ in us, feeding the deep root of the will; Christ, giving himself to be our self.

For we must use figures and parables; but how they mislead! The parables of grace - and we have Christ's own authority for them - speak of the branch drawing sap from the vine, and the seed building the plant from the materials of soil and rain. But grace is no process of nature, no ray of light kindling into flame, no soil or water feeding a vegetable root; it is the sheer bounty of God.

Said or Sung, pp. 109, 110

129

PENTECOST 9

=

Mind Flows into Mind

I couldn't seriously pray for my friends if I thought I was merely exercising my kinder desires, by dwelling on their names with affection. I have to believe that it does them some good. Very well; but you *can* believe it. And now I'm going to surprise, and if possible, shock you. I'm going to talk about spiritualism. What can spiritualistic mediums do? Can they communicate with the departed? No, there is no evidence that they can. But there is so much evidence that it is silly to dispute it, of their receiving into their minds masses of material out of the hearts and memories of the living, with which they recreate the images of departed persons unknown to themselves by ordinary acquaintance. Now spiritualistic mediums are freaks: but they are not absolute freaks. It is very unscientific, indeed, to believe in absolute freaks anywhere in nature. Freaks are special developments of common characteristics. Mind does everywhere flow into mind. How it happens is neither here nor there: it happens. Spiritualism teaches its votaries to make a forced and abnormal use of this power, a use leading to illusion. True religion teaches us the true use of it; and that use is nothing else but intercession. We place our hearts at the disposal of God's will, to spread that influence which he has placed in us in support of our friends' happiness or virtue. We don't have to think a lot of ourselves, or of our spiritual powers, to do that; for influence will flow from us in any case; only, if it is not submitted to God's direction it will be as likely to be bad as good, depressing as uplifting.

A Celebration of Faith, pp. 143, 144

Psychic Contact

To say that the psychically weird belongs to the bottom of the soul is
not of course to deny that it may be made the instrument of noble acts
and purposes. After all, what most of the weird phenomena amount to
is roughly this, that whereas we used to think that our minds touched
the rest of the world through our own bodies alone, we may now have
to admit that they touch it at many other points besides: and especially
that our minds touch one another without bodily intervention. If this is
a fact, it is just a fact about the way in which the multitude of finite
things jostle one another in one universe. As there is nothing specially
godlike in the fact that our bodies touch, so there is nothing specially
godlike in the fact (if it is a fact) of our spirits touching. Physical contact
is nothing godlike, and yet through physical contact a compassionate
will can perform those acts which will redeem it from everlasting fire
and set it on the right hand of the divine Shepherd - to feed the hungry,
to clothe the naked and to visit the captive. So psychical contact will be
merely contact, yet of what may not it be made the instrument? Christians
believe that their acts of prayer may, under God, assist their neighbours'
souls, and it seems likely that the touch of mind on mind has something
to do with that. Christians believe also that the charity of departed saints
can assist us in this world, and our prayers assist the departed in their
purgation: there is an interchange of spiritual act among the members
of Christ's body, as though all, in some way, touched one another. There
is certainly something godlike here, but it is not the touching, it is what
the touching is made to convey - supernatural charity. The exercise of
the praying act is god-like, not the contact by which it affects (if it does
so affect) another's mind: that is mere mechanics, and might be the
vehicle of bad influence as well as good. We pray with the apex of the
mind, with the intelligent will, with what we have always known to be
the very principle of our selfhood. And if, in praying, we reach above
the apex into what, transcending our nature, is supernatural to us, it is
not in touching our neighbours, it is in touching God.

The Glass of Vision, pp. 27, 28

The Cunning against Us

It is a popular aphorism that the devil's cleverest manoeuvre was inducing us to disbelieve in him. The meaning of the remark is that we shall be ill-prepared to resist an undermining corruption which we are persuaded to ignore. And there is practical truth in this, if the alternative to a belief in Satan is an ill-founded confidence in our own rational processes. To deny Satan may be to suppose that we have nothing to fear from detached psychic forces in our own souls or in other men's; forces which may wear the guise of a subhuman malice and of an instinctive cunning; forces of which the minds housing them may be largely unaware. To ignore such forces is certainly dangerous and it is better to call them 'Satan' than to disbelieve in them. But suppose we do believe in them, and, not content with believing, wish to understand them. We shall follow their action better if we view it as a sort of cunning, than if we view it as a sort of natural force. Only, in the interpretation of the cunning, we shall be largely led astray if we call it Satanic; if we see it as the strategy of a rebel archangel, set single-mindedly on the damnation of souls. There is available to us a mythology somewhat less dogmatic, though scarcely less luxuriant, worked out by psychologists with their eye a little more closely on the facts.

We all know the difficulty of proving a universal negative by particular evidence. It seemed clear that there were no black swans, until someone went to Australia and found them there. It is a good rhetorical point to ask, 'How do you know that there are no spirts who, like wicked men, have revolted from God? And how do you know that they never poke a finger into our affairs?' We shall be forced to reply that we cannot possibly be certain of either negative. But equally, there may be pink elephants and blue kangaroos on a habitable planet somewhere in the galaxies; who is to deny it? Only we shall not trouble our heads with the possibility, until we have evidence of the fact.

Love Almighty and Ills Unlimited, pp. 147, 148

PENTECOST 10

===

Living with God

We must pray, for prayer is neither more nor less than living with God. Shall I live today of myself and by myself, or shall I live it with God? Doubtless, whether or not I live it with God, God lives it with me – but that only makes it the more monstrous that I should not live it with him. Prayer is just living with God: looking at him, regarding his will, reaching out our hands for the blessings he is so eager to give, bringing our action into his. We must pray. If you cannot pray, come and ask for help. What could be more natural, than for a Christian to say to a priest, may I make a date to talk to you about my prayers? What else are we for?

The End of Man, p. 106

133

Christ the Underlying Cause of Our Thinking

I should now like to ask how important it is deemed to be that the philosopher's experience should fall into the form of an inward colloquy, with one part of his thought addressing another as though with the voice of God. I have a special and personal interest in challenging the colloquy-form, because of an obstacle I remember encountering in my own adolescence. . . I thought of myself as set over against deity as one man faces another across a table, except that God was invisible and indefinitely great. And I hoped that he would signify his presence to me by way of colloquy; but neither out of the Scripture I read nor in the prayers I tried to make did any mental voice address me. I believe at that time anything would have satisfied me, but nothing came: no 'other' stood beside me, no shadow of presence fell upon me. I owe my liberation from this *impasse*, as far as I can remember, to reading Spinoza's *Ethics*.

I would no longer attempt, with the psalmist, 'to set God before my face'. I would see him as the underlying cause of my thinking, especially of those thoughts in which I tried to think of him. I would dare to hope that sometimes my thought would become diaphanous, so that there should be some perception of the divine cause shining through the created effect, as a deep pool, settling into a clear tranquillity, permits us to see the spring in the bottom of it from which its waters rise.

Such things, I say, I dared to hope for, and I will not say that my hope was in any way remarkably fulfilled, but I will say that by so viewing my attempted work of prayer, I was rid of the frustration which had baffled me before. And this is why, when Germans set their eyeballs and pronounce the terrific words 'He speaks to thee' (*Er redet dich an*) I am sure, indeed, that they are saying something, but I am still more sure that they are not speaking to my condition.

The Glass of Vision, p. 7

The Prayer of His Heart

Father Almighty, Maker of heaven and earth, what shall we give you, what have we that you desire? You desire our love and you desire to do us good, and these two desires are one. For if we turn to you in love we shall receive you into ourselves, and if we admit you into ourselves you will do us all the good you have prepared for us. You desire that we should put back into your hands all that your love has made us, in longing after all that your love will make of us, and in adoration of all that your love is. I can say the words, I cannot do the thing: I am not the master of my heart. What I give I give with part of my mind, and what I give now I shall take back in half an hour. My rooted longing is after vanity and pleasure; I love your love little, my mind being mostly turned from it. Father Almighty, look upon and receive the only acceptable offering, the love of your beloved Son. Regard this prayer of ours not as it is in us, but as it is in him, who prays it in hope ahead of us, and in sympathy along with us. In us it is an episode, a patch of gold cloth on a threadbare garment; in him it is all of one piece with his life and his death, it is that part of his heart which embraces us. This prayer, even in our praying it, shall not be ours; we will go into the heart of Jesus Christ. We will dare, as well as we can do, to be your blessed Son, praying for your Name to be hallowed, your Kingdom to come, your will to be done. We will explore the cares of his heart for his Church, and for our friends, and for our perfection.

Lord I Believe, p. 40

135

PENTECOST 11

Theme of the Week: The Serving Community

———

Still in the Making

What commands the theist's moral response is the divine will expressed in his neighbour's being. Our neighbour is a piece of the divine handiwork, still in the making; it is the process of creation still continuing, which demands our instrumental cooperation. God (it is the theist's belief) is making our neighbour. And yet our neighbour is, in some measure at least, making himself. The same thing is true, we suppose, of ourselves; a providence shapes us, and it is this very work of God upon us, which commands our obedience in the ordering of our lives.

The Freedom of the Will, p. 310

Fighting the Causes of Pain

If we say that God, from the motive of compassion, should have spared his creatures all suffering, we are surely talking nonsense. It is only because God allots pain that there is any object for his compassion, or any sense in speaking of it.

But the greatest fallacy in this whole field has still to be mentioned. This is the suggestion that God's assigning of pain, if admitted, provides a reason why we should harden our hearts. On the contrary; every pain God assigns is a call to us to remove the cause of it. God does not give pains that they may be passively endured; he gives them to awaken our detestation of their causes.

He provokes us to fight the causes; he cannot, within the fabric of the existing world, prevent their arising. It must never be forgotten that God is the God of hawks no less than of sparrows, of microbes no less than of men. He saves his creatures by creating in them the power to meet the ever-changing hostilities of their environment. And so, though individuals perish and species die out, there is a world of life.

Love Almighty and Ills Unlimited, pp. 104, 105

Even in Tragedy a Will to Be Done

God works everything into his further purposes, for his work never ceases; and he always goes on from the actual situation into which things have come. Everything gets worked into God's further purposes. So God brings much good out of much evil; much good that we cannot recognize, but a considerable range that we can. The flow of lava which drives the villagers from their cottages will enrich their fields, as it crumbles, with an unparalleled fertility. The earthquake which destroys the town calls forth in some victims heroic virtue and teaches others to know their own weakness. People in the surrounding cities are shaken out of their usual selfishness and give so much in relief that they halve their cigar-smoking, or put off the purchase of a shinier car for eighteen months; a moral triumph indeed.

It cannot be disputed that such sorts of good are born out of disaster; but the disaster is a disaster still. Healthy and useful lives are lost to the earth. Earth's loss is heaven's gain, no doubt; but couldn't heaven have waited? Sane people forfeit their reason, cripples linger on, horribly maimed; to save their lives or their possessions, decent men commit acts of unspeakable meanness, which stain their conscience for the rest of their lives; some become embittered, some can never find their feet again when the ground on which they so comfortably stood is cut from under them.

It is not, then, that the humanly inconvenient by-products of volcanic fire are cushioned or diverted; it is not that all harms to man are prevented. It is that the creative work of God never ceases, that there is always something his providence does, even for the most tragically stricken. There is always a will of God to be sought in any situation, however, unpromising – to be sought by our minds, that it may be served by our hands.

A Science of God?, pp. 89, 90

137

PENTECOST 12

No Rest for Our Thinking

It remains that the act of thinking the divine perfection strains to the uttermost the powers of the human mind. How could it be otherwise, if God is God? In this act there is no rest; to think of the divine perfection is always to have taken our start from various and impure finitude and to be in the process of purifying and simplifying it in the direction of the absolute and the one. But we have never arrived; as we seem on the point to do so, our thought evaporates in the emptiness of mathematical unity, or, as happens to some, passes into an ecstasy and ceases to be thinking. If we wish to think on, we must return humbly to the bottom of the ladder, and climb again.

In this act there is no rest - no rest for our faculties, for the discoursing mind. And yet there is rest for the spirit, which through the act of discourse maintains contact with that which alters not, and acquiesces in it.

Finite and Infinite, pp. 60, 61

138

Prayer for One Another

Jesus is himself the perfect pattern of a true self-reliance. He walks through the pages of the Gospel serene and master of the event. What worldly man would guess the secret of his submissive sonship, his entire dependence? Nowhere is this more striking than in Gethsemane, where in a moment of sudden armed surprise he presented so calm a front to the ambushers, it was they, you might have thought, not he, on whom the trap had been sprung.

Yet what lay behind? Jesus sweating blood and tears to find, embrace and follow his Father's will. Nor was his recourse to his Father only; he scorned no aid, but drew his childish disciples round him, that they might add their prayers to his. I know it is possible to dispute this interpretation – to hold that the disciples were only to pray for themselves, not for him; but heart and reason alike revolt against the artificial limitation. When men kneel together to pray in common danger, the traffic of mutual help runs in every direction, there are no artificial barriers; all pray for all, their prayer is one.

Said or Sung, p. 55

Double Thinking

You *think* you believe; but you are deceived. You are a double thinker: you have two systems of thinking which in fact you keep apart – you think, as people say, in watertight compartments. And when you switch from one system of your thinking to another, that is, from your religious thinking to your practical thinking, you turn a blind eye to the transition, the passage from the world of reality to the world of fantasy. In the world of reality you think like anyone else (unless, of course, you are a lunatic or a fanatic). But when you turn to your devotions, or read pious books, you enjoy a fantasy picture of the world as subject to God's goodness and governed by his providence. And in this fantasy picture of the world there is a fantasy picture of yourself as a Christian, mysteriously incorporate with Christ and serving his cause, with only occasional lapses and deviations. Whereas in fact you are just an undergraduate or a business man, or some other type of worldly man, a serious man, perhaps a virtuous man, but one who does not take the will of God into his practical calculations, or experience his life as conducted by God. That is just a story you amuse yourself with while you are worshipping or praying or talking pious talk.

Well, now I think you will see what the accusation of double thinking amounts to: and I think also that you will see how deeply the accusation bites into our consciences, and how important it is that we should lay it to heart. For which of us Christians is there, whose conscience does not reproach him bitterly with the crime of double thinking, or, as Christ himself called it, the crime of hypocrisy? For hypocrisy, as attacked by Christ, does not mean self-conscious humbug, it means just 'play acting', that is to say, that the religion of the hypocrite no more enters into the rest of his life than the part the player acts on the stage enters into his life off the stage. In fact, Christ meant by hypocrisy what is now called 'double thinking', the endemic disease of religion everywhere.

To the clever logicians, Christianity is an amiable and harmless hypocrisy. But we take the thing more seriously. Christian hypocrisy is not amiable or harmless at all. We are all hypocrites, indeed, because we are all sinners, but God is saving us out of our hypocrisy, if we are faithful to him: he is forcing the two parts of our thinking together. That is the whole issue in the religious life, not to be a double thinker, or anyhow, to be less and less of one.

A Celebration of Faith, pp. 27, 28

PENTECOST 13

—

His Will that They Should Be Themselves

The way to study God's mind in nature is to let things show us how they go. No doubt God's providence will also work their natural action into higher designs; but we have seldom any reason to trust our guesses as to what these higher designs may be. Those who start from a rash confidence in such guesses, instead of starting from a patient study of natural processes, land themselves in that terrible morass of muddled thinking which goes by the name 'the problem of suffering'. If an earthquake shakes down a city, an urgent practical problem arises – how to rescue, feed, house and console the survivors, rehabilitate the injured, and commend the dead to the mercy of God; less immediately, how to reconstruct in a way which will minimize the effects of another such disaster. But no theological problem arises. The will of God expressed in the event is his will for the physical elements in the earth's crust or under it: his will that they should go on being themselves and acting in accordance with their natures.

What would happen to the system of nature if God did habitually overrule, is too terrible to contemplate. Fortunately he does not overrule; he uses, or in some mysterious way persuades. Does God use the crust and undercrust of the earth for man's benefit? Does he lead or persuade physical elements present there into structural combinations on which human life is built? Certainly; that is just what he does do – always supposing that there is a God of nature at all. The success of biological life requires that the earth's crust should for the most part have cooled and settled. If the process had gone so far that there was no risk either of earthquake or volcano, it might be too cool for us altogether; snow and ice would win the day, as no doubt they will at last, when there has been enough of human history.

A Science of God?, pp. 87, 88, 89

141

God's Mysterious Hands

I don't know whether you ever try to read the Book of Job. If so, what do you make of it? It is the description of a mental agony; as for the solution, and the happy ending, one can't help feeling that it has been clamped on by violence, like a happy ending added to *Hamlet* by an old-fashioned film producer. But what of Job's mental agony? For modern taste, it seems too much concerned with a worry about wicked men escaping their punishment, and righteous men failing of their reward: and most of us don't care whether the wicked are punished or not (except of course when the wicked attack us) nor yet whether the just are or are not rewarded (except, of course, when we see ourselves in the role of good men lacking due recognition). But really the whole question of kicks and halfpence is very superficial. It is, of course, meat and drink to Job's comforters, but Job has a deeper concern. Job has loved God, and wants to love him still: even more, he wants to have God loving him. But how can this be? God's love was shown in flocks and herds, in sons and daughters, and no less in the good and useful life he gave Job to live, as a magistrate and a patron of the poor. But one day has carried off the herds, killed the children and brought Job down from the seat of judgement to the dunghill. We can love no other God but a God revealed in his acts; and the love of God to us is itself action, no mere sentiment. Job is as a man whose friend has stabbed him – *Et tu, Brute?* – even now he would love God, if he could see any sense in it, if someone could show him why God should have done it.

It is no accident that the solution of the plot is no solution of the problem: without the revelation of Christ, there is no escape from Job's dilemma. If we are to love God, we must feel him in the whole substance of our life: we cannot love disembodied ghosts, and the whole world pressing in on us is the body, or better, let us say, the hand, through which God upholds, directs, checks and caresses us. And without Christ's revelation of redemptive suffering, and everlasting life, we should lack the voice which interprets to us the action of God's mysterious hands.

A Celebration of Faith, pp. 173, 174

Pains out of Love for Them

God does not want his creatures for any ulterior aim; he wants them to be, for their sakes, not his. Not, indeed, only for the sake of each creature, taken severally; he wants it also to serve or feed or delight or propagate others; but it ministers to these aims indirectly, and by being itself first. . .

Let it be assumed that God cares for the sparrow. What form will his caring take? He will lovingly and heedfully benefit her. And how? By his creative action, by his continual sustenance and direction of her natural life. And this will be imperceptible to us, except in so far as it is manifest in the working of nature.

When Christ appealed to God's feeding of the ravens, or his clothing of the grass, he was not citing special providences. The tale of Elijah asserted that God had once made ravens carry miraculous loaves to feed the prophet. The Sermon on the Mount does not mean anything like the provision of miraculous loaves through prophetic hands, to feed the ravens. They are fed through the common ecology of nature. The things on which they feed flourish in their feeding grounds; and they have the wit, or the instinct, to feed on them.

The God of nature gives his animal creatures pains out of love for them, to save their lives; he makes the way of destruction distasteful to them, as a parent makes the path of danger distasteful to a child, by little punishments. Again, out of love for them, God moves his creatures to shun their pains and mend their harms, so far as their sense or capacity allows. And at last, when they must acknowledge defeat, as every perishable creature must, he relieves them of the power and will to struggle, of the pain on stimulus of which they can no longer usefully act, and of the being they can no longer hopefully defend.

Love Almighty and Ills Unlimited, pp. 101, 102

143

===

Mothers

My sisters and I were born in Hampstead, and were brought up by a mother who was so dependable, she was almost like a piece of God's nature herself. The house always went smoothly. There was very little money behind it, but somehow no one was allowed to feel the strain. There were always good meals on time – my mother got very tired, I believe, but she did it somehow. She soothed everyone's troubles and never mentioned her own. If she had made more fuss, I suppose I should have taken more notice: if I had had to do without her, I should have seen what I owed to her. Her goodness made me thoughtless. I remember once thinking it would be fun to drive home from Oxford with three fellow students, who were going far and so wanted to start very early. 'We'll stop at our place,' I said, 'and have breakfast.' I rang my mother up at some terrible hour in the morning and we all landed hungry on the mat. The breakfast was there and my mother smiled. It was only years afterwards that she recalled the occasion, and laughed at me for having been so absurd. She had had practically nothing in the larder.

And so it is the faithfulness of God, his unseen dependableness, which makes us ungrateful. 'Ah, my dear Mother,' I can now say, 'how I wish . . .' – but it is too late.

My mother was a good woman – no one more truly a Christian – and I dare say she did not specially want to be made a fuss of, or to hear endless speeches of thanks. She wanted her children to grow and thrive on her kindness, to work along with her efforts in bringing us up. There is a sort of unthankfulness which is far more cruel than an unthankful tongue – and that is, a contempt for people's services to us. Is a cook more hurt by our lack of praise, or by our leaving her food uneaten? The worst ungratefulness to parents is, not asking for their help, not taking their advice; if they give us presents of clothes, not wearing them; if they give us presents of books, not reading them.

So it is with God. The real unthankfulness is pushing away the things he wants to give us most.

The End of Man, pp. 54, 55

Union of Soul and Body

St Paul makes a most curious remark. 'Every sin that a man commits', he says, 'is without his body; but he who sins with woman sins against his own body.' What does the apostle mean? Is murder committed without involving one's body in the act? And isn't gluttony a sin against one's own body, which it degrades by the practice and weakens by the effect? But if we look at the context, we can see that St Paul is speaking in a very special sense. By 'sin involving the body' he means 'sin tying up one's person with another person, so that the two persons become inseparable'. This is the only sin, he says, which involves that special sort of tie-up. What he is saying is that you cannot have it both ways. If the union of the sexes in marriage is a unique personal bond, then the union of the sexes outside marriage is a parody of that bond. If marriage is a sacrament, promiscuity must be a sacrilege. And he emphasizes this consideration by invoking the mysterious comparison between our spiritual marriage with Christ, and our bodily marriage with one another.

So many miserable reasons have been found for our behaving ourselves, and by contrast the biblical reason is so splendid. When St Paul was writing to his still half-heathen Corinthians, all the reasons which have been current in worldly minds from then till now had already been found. The philosophers were saying, Passion is base, starve it; reason is noble, foster it; but the Bible has nothing to do with this sort of cultural snobbery. Lawyers were laying it down that wives are property not to be purloined, and marriageable girls marketable commodities not to be spoilt. Moses may speak in this strain, but Christ does not. Social utilitarians were pointing out how undesirable it is for fatherless children to get loose in the world. But the Bible never refers to this unquestionable nuisance as a reason to be chaste. No, the faith of Christ takes its stand on the integrity of the human person. We are to move in one piece, body, heart and spirit, and not to commit our body to the other until we commit our heart and soul in an entire and permanent union.

Said or Sung, pp. 175, 176

PENTECOST 15

———

The Otherness of God

We are perfectly clear that for us there is a positive and practical value in asserting the otherness of God. For it means that we exercise our relation with him as a personal relation. God is not, indeed, out there in space beside us, like one of our neighbours; he is at the causal root of our being, and of every being; and it is through our root (to maintain the metaphor) that we receive his grace. But his otherness for us lies in this, that his life is personal to him, it is not ours; that he has a will after which we inquire, a judgement to which we submit, a forgiveness we implore, a succour we seek; that the personal character of our relation with him is the very form of it, not a metaphorical trapping which can be thought away while any substance remains.

Faith and Speculation, p. 47

146

The Strength of Tradition

Keble, then, accepted his tradition and struck his roots deep into the soil of family, country and Church. The principle of his being was piety, as much in the old Roman as in the modern Christian sense. He was a lover and an acceptor, not a critic. The Church of Hooker and Laud was founded on Scripture and the Fathers: and back, back into the Fathers, and into Scripture, Keble pushed the fibres of his mind. The stuff of the good tradition was all splendour and divinity; the faces in his family background were all as bright as angels. This dear and humble man saw Christ everywhere in his Christian relatives, his tutors, pupils, friends; only in his own heart he saw an unilluminated emptiness; and yet he knew, for all his ceaseless penitence, that he had the grace of God, and that he was forgiven.

He was, to start with, a kind son and brother, and a heavenly friend; and it was the supernatural overflow of such natural kindness on to all sorts of people, that made him the excellent pastor he was. He spent the last thirty years of his life in Hursley parish, indefatigable in teaching the children, visiting the sick, recalling the impenitent, bearing all his parishioners in his heart, always interceding, supplying everyone's every need, answering with his own hand letters in request of religious direction, which flowed to him from every side. He was able to do all this work in company; he scarcely saw his study, except for solemn interviews. He could do his work with a pleasant smile, and many interventions in the conversation, sitting with his wife and her friends in the drawing room.

The Brink of Mystery, p. 150

The Authority of the Church

The Church of England is not *the* Church; there is only one Church, as there is only one Christ. The centre of the Church is neither Rome nor Canterbury; it is the heart of Heaven. There is a company of saints who enjoy the society of Jesus Christ more intimately than his disciples ever did on earth. We, who only know him by faith and touch him only in sacraments, are no more than outposts and colonies of his sacred empire.

Meanwhile, how can I, truly and with a good conscience, abide in the Church of God? Only by remaining in the Church of England. But why? Because the people there are visibly the most pious, or the missionary action visibly the most efficacious, the ceremonies the most dignified or the most congenial? No. It is not for me to admire or embrace, or even prefer, a sect called Anglicanism. What is it then? There are two overriding considerations. I dare not dissociate myself from the apostolic ministry, and the continuous sacramental life of the Church extending unbroken from the first days until now. That is the first point, and the second is this: I dare not profess belief in the great papal error. Christ did not found a papacy. No such institution appeared for several hundred years. Its infallibilist claim is a blasphemy, and never has been accepted by the oriental part of Christendom. Its authority has been employed to establish as dogmas of faith, propositions utterly lacking in historical foundation. Nor is this an old or faded scandal - the papal fact-factory has been going full blast in our own time, manufacturing sacred history after the event.

I cannot desert the apostolic ministry, I cannot submit to the Pope. And I was not born a Greek or Slavic Christian. I was born in this English-speaking world, where God's merciful providence has preserved the form and substance of the Catholic Church, and freed it from papal usurpation.

The End of Man, pp. 50, 51

PENTECOST 16

===

What Is the Lord Showing Us?

The grand error about intellectual integrity is the belief that it can be achieved by limitation of view: by scrupulous care in cleaning out the moat of an ivory tower, or cultivating the hedges round a fool's paradise. There can be no integrity about refusing to pronounce on things from which we avert our eyes. Integrity of mind is the acknowledgement of truth. The first step is not to avert our eyes from anything. The second is to tell the truth, as well as we can, here and now, about what the Lord God is showing us.

Ah, but what is the Lord God showing us? . . . He is the maker of heaven and earth, and a million stars proclaim his glory; so do a million motes dancing in the sunbeams. I cannot attend to all these things at once, so to what shall I attend? I will choose the objects of my attention. So Dives thought (if we may venture to elaborate Christ's parable). He chose to be an expert in what advertisers call 'gracious living'. No one so scientific, so honest and exact a judge of *objets d'art* and vintages as he. Lazarus was not included in his subject. Beggars, dogs and flies were everywhere; if you started attending to that sort of thing, where would you stop?

But a man who cannot understand that a dying beggar has more claim on his attention than a Chinese vase, has not solved the problem of intellectual integrity. He does not know where the truth is which claims to be acknowledged, if he can shut his eyes at Lazarus and not feel the fingers of God pulling them open. Without a sense of what is important and what is not, we have nothing to be sincere about, or even to be insincere about, either. Sincerity in the pursuit of self-chosen hobbies is trivial. It would not save Dives from everlasting fire, and it will not save us. We have to be sincere in the acknowledgement of what the Lord God is showing us.

Said or Sung, pp. 172, 173

The Claims upon Us

I am responsible. But what sort of responsibility is this? Surely the original metaphor of law has become so stretched, that it has lost the substance of meaning. To whom, or what, am I now said to be responsible? Not, surely, to my own mind, as to an authority which has fulminated the law I have neglected; for that is just what my mind has failed to do. I may still be called upon to be my own executioner; but I have not been my own legislator. No; if any comparison with the citizen under law remains, it will probably be this: that just as the statutes have been fulminated by authority, and it is the responsibility of John Doe or Richard Roe to acknowledge them; so moral claims are shouted at me by the very existence of my neighbours, and it is my responsibility to acknowledge such claims. But facts do not shout, not even personal facts; they have no voices. All they can do, or need do, is to be important for practical decision. What has the word 'responsibility' to do here? All it does is to call attention to a characteristic of certain ranges of importance, or of value; that their claim to be recognized is not optional, but obligatory. If you say to me, that there is an important play at the theatre, and that I must not miss it, you exaggerate. I can miss it if I like; and by giving it a miss, I discredit neither its dramatic merit, nor my own sincerity in accepting your estimate of it. I agree that the play is interesting, significant, what you will; but I am in no mood for plays. Whereas if Lazarus is dying on the doorstep, Dives is free neither to deny the importance of the fact, nor, if he concedes it, to keep his hands in his pockets. That the values of human life, virtue, and happiness lie upon us with a unique incumbency is evident; and what else is meant, by saying that we are *responsible* for doing something about them?

The Freedom of the Will, pp. 275, 276

Multiplication of the Image

The love which consists of preference may be difficult, but at least it is intelligible; the love which is delight may seem not even intelligible; for what could be meant by delighting in God above all things? And if any one does it, is it not some enraptured mystic? And would it not be mere hypocrisy for me to pretend that I even want to be such a person? But let me consider these words: 'The light of the glorious gospel of Jesus Christ, who is the image of God.' If I cannot delight more than a moment here and there in God, yet I may constantly delight in his image. For as God sent his Son into the world to be his speaking image, so this Son has multiplied the image everywhere. God is to be loved in his Son, and his Son is to be loved in all the human race. 'Inasmuch', he says, 'as ye have done it to the least of these my brethren, ye have done it to me.' And again, 'He that welcomes me welcomes him that sent me.'

Said or Sung, p. 49

Starting Again

As for us, the reality of our faith is not tested by our achievement hitherto, but by our repentance now. We have nothing, or virtually nothing, to show in the way of performance: our personal religion is a poor thing. But are we sorry, and are we willing to obey the indwelling God now, with such heart and strength as we have, to identify ourselves with Christ's love of God and Christ's care for our neighbours, to yield to his Holy Spirit? The promises we make to God, though they be sincere, will be forgotten and broken, but the next time we remember, we can repent and renew the offering of our service.

And so it is possible for us to have faith even in a God indwelling us, by virtue of two things: our part with Jesus Christ and the saints in one Catholic Church on earth and in heaven; and our own daily repentance, our constantly renewed submission, our humble prayer and faithful endeavour.

The Brink of Mystery, p. 17

PENTECOST 17

—

The Root of Our Being

God acts by simple will; and we cannot see the will of God except in what that will has created. There is only one point at which we can possibly touch the nerve of God's creative action, or experience creation taking place: and that is in our own life. The believer draws his active Christian existence out of the wellspring of divine creation, he prays prayers which become the very act of God's will in his will. Because we have God under the root of our being we cannot help but acknowledge him at the root of all the world's being. So it is that, where the atheist sees the search for an ultimate explanation of things as a meaningless 'Why?', we see it as the searching out of God's creative power.

A Celebration of Faith, pp. 60, 61

Take Their Criticism to Heart

Since God has shown to me a ray of his goodness, I cannot doubt him on the ground that someone has made up some new logical puzzles about him. It is too late in the day to tell me that God does not exist, the God with whom I have so long conversed, and whom I have seen active in several living men of real sanctity, not to mention the canonized saints. But there must be much in our teaching of Christianity and our living of it which is at fault, if good men react in total disbelief of it. So let us open our ears to what they say, and take the implied criticism to heart.

A Celebration of Faith, p. 27

What Is Most Worthy of Love?

What is the supreme motive of a truth-seeking mind? Is it to explode shams, or to acknowledge realities? And now suppose that there are realities supremely important, but at the same time too intangible to be proved, will intellectual honesty discount them, or will it embrace them?

It is a commonplace to say that many things are acceptable to faith, which are not accessible to certain knowledge. This is true as far as it goes - faith is an act or attitude by which we put trust in things unproved by knock-down evidence, but we still want to know the motive on which faith acts. Faith is not its own motive, or ought not to be. We do not want people going about with a sheer appetite for indiscriminate believing. But faith, in the Christian sense, is the twin of love. And love, with its inexhaustible appetite for what deserves loving, sees beyond evidence, sees the soul behind the body, and God behind all. Then faith comes into play - faith, the act of the will, by which we determine to accept, or to worship, or to trust, what draws our love.

But though faith and love go beyond absolute evidence, they are not blind. If we really love and trust another person, we do not wish to entertain a fantastic image of what they are, especially not of their thoughts or desires; and the saint has similarly a fine sensitivity for the revealed mind of God.

After all the detection of shams, the clarification of argument, and the sifting of evidence - after all criticism, all analysis - a man must make up his mind what there is most worthy of love, and most binding on conduct, in the world of real existence. It is this decision, or this discovery, that is the supreme exercise of a truthseeking intelligence.

The End of Man, pp. 156, 157

The Proof in Our Life

When the logicians say that there is a certain inevitable division between spiritual thinking and natural thinking, they are in a certain sense right. We can't reconcile the spiritual picture of things and the everyday picture of things completely on the intellectual level. If we claimed to be able to do it, we should claim to comprehend the ways of God as well as we comprehend the ways of this world, and that would be an exaggerated claim. We see God in pictures, in images only, reflected in a glass and riddlingly says St Paul: and we cannot fuse our picture of God perfectly with our picture of the natural world. There always remains a certain discontinuity, a certain incoherence on the intellectual level.

The saints confute the logicians, but they do not confute them by logic but by sanctity. They do not prove the real connection between the religious symbols and the everyday realities by logical demonstration, but by life. It is solved by sacrifice. I can offer my life to the God who has shown me his face in the glass of riddles. The God who is seen in the sphere of religion takes control in the sphere of conduct, and there he gives me, unworthy, the help of his holy spirit.

You can live your religion if you like; you can know the reality of God if you like: for God will rejoice to assist and infinitely over-reward whatever effort you will make. *Resolution* is the crucial point. That is the link by which religious contemplation passes into practical action. From your prayers form simple resolutions – not, like the absurd resolutions of New Year's Day, resolutions for the next twelve months; but resolutions for the next twelve hours. Make them few enough to be practicable, and obey them for the sake of God himself. If you break them, repeat and renew them. 'What does God ask of me?' is a part of every sincere prayer. By resolutions kept, men turn religious fantasy into the substance of living. By resolutions broken, men learn their weakness and are driven back on God. By resolutions renewed and kept they learn to live by him who says: 'My strength is made perfect in weakness' and 'my grace is sufficient for thee.'

A Celebration of Faith, pp. 29, 30

PENTECOST 18

Theme of the Week: The Offering of Life

——

Money Is Power

It is good to give riches away - not because money is a bad thing: charity isn't like the hot penny in the children's game, which you pass on as fast as you can from hand to hand, since you are to lose a forfeit if you are caught holding it. No, the reason against holding much money is that money is power, money is opportunity, and your poor neighbours haven't got enough of it. Money is a serious subject. There is nothing more bogus than that affectation of aristocratic high-mindedness which considers the weighing of expenses to be beneath notice, and the paying of tailors' bills to be a bourgeois scruple.

The End of Man, p. 82

The Dynamo of the Heart

The God who made us is not unaware of the fact he permitted Sigmund Freud to discover that man, dynamically viewed, is a sexual animal. Therefore, having raised us to the capacity of fellowship with himself, this God, whom Moses dares to call jealous, is determined to capture the dynamo of our heart, our basic fund of emotional force, and turn it to his service. He has prescribed two ways. There is the hard way, where the sublimation or redirection of sexual force is complete. And in answer to the charge, that those who tread this path are unattractive figures, we can only put forward the radiant holiness of Jesus Christ, and of those virginal saints whom supernatural charity has wholly possessed. An inability to appreciate such splendours merely convicts of blindness the beholder. Happy are they who have known such men, or such women, face to face. Yet the calling is for few, and most of us, trying to follow it, would be miserable, or frustrated. Nor would the purposes of God be served; since he also loves and fosters the nature he has made.

Nevertheless our Creator will not surrender his claim upon any one of us. He will not have any of us knot so tying a bond, so intimate and exclusive an association as fleshly union is, except with the person whom we can receive from his own hands, and under his own law, and for his own purposes. A husband or wife is given us as the deputy of Christ himself, to be loved with as entire and as exclusive a loyalty. So marriage becomes a sacrament of religion, and a speaking likeness of our union with our Redeemer.

The Brink of Mystery, pp. 131-2

156

Time for What?

I suppose it is right that God desires most men to follow the decent and humdrum occupations we propose to follow, or how is the world to go on? And for the present we are in this University. Let us accept that God means us to be here, but let us go on to see how he means us to live here. We shall never know God unless we listen for him, and let him direct us. He will tell us very simple things, and he will tell us them again and again: to make a proper job of our work – to go out of our way to be encouraging to dull and discouraged people – to control our lustful hearts – to manage our lives sensibly, so that we can sleep, communicate and pray – to live with our friends for their pleasure, not for our own glory: to do important things first and attractive things second. God will teach us these simple lessons again and again. He will also bring into our minds particular duties, and make us see particular needs. There is no religion, and no escape from unreality, without God's will.

But perhaps it is not all God asks of us, to be faithful in our present station. Since we spare so much time for recreation, perhaps he asks us to spare a little for something more in the line of what St Vincent and his helpers did. There are hospitals to be visited, lonely and housebound old people to be befriended, jobs of manual work to be done for those who cannot themselves do them. The doing or not doing of such things, like every other decision, should be referred to the will of God. How can I best use my time in this world? That is our question before the face of God. One day we shall have eternity to play with, but now we've only got time, and it's a perishing commodity. Let us receive it and use it as from the hands of God.

A Celebration of Faith, p. 201

PENTECOST 19

=

Finding Him Now

Who taste thy goodness hunger still,
Who drink thee cannot drink their fill.

Qui te gustant, esuriunt;
Qui bibunt, adhuc sitiunt;

and those who have found God, still have God to find, every morning
when they go to pray, and every evening when they come to repent.
God has to be found, over and over again; for he keeps seeming not to
be there. Why is this? Because the very air we breathe is worldliness,
and worldliness is only another name for practical atheism, or counting
God out. Jesus told his disciples to abide in him, and saints have made
it their endeavour never for a moment to forget the presence of God.
Yet for most of us the world is too strong, and life with God has
immense gaps in it. Our 'abiding' in him is, at best, a certain elasticity
in springing back to him. We must find our base, our abiding-place,
again and again: and, as often as not, it looks as if it can't be found.

We can never live on our past: we have always to find God here and
now, and nothing else matters but our finding him *this* time.

The Brink of Mystery, p. 140

158

Care for the Sparrow

God is no less concerned for the individual, than for the future of the species. The life and activity of the single thrush or squirrel or grasshopper is a work of God.

The miracle of the total evolutionary process, from its rudimentary beginnings to its highest visible development, is a manifestation of creative power. But to a sensitive mind, the miracle of the individual creature is just as striking and no less divine. Every sparrow is its own little self; it is no mere complex of general principles in combined action. God has made, and continues to make it. But here, as in the wider field, he works through natural forces and natural characteristics. Looking at the unique individuality and singular life story of any creature, we shall be unable to distinguish what comes by mere animal nature from the touch of divine direction imparted to it. Any fact or feature we can sufficiently isolate to ask why it is there will always appear to have a natural cause. The hand of God is perfectly hidden.

So God cares for the sparrow. Each bird is his particular creation, her vital effort a unique drama of his composition. But no natural regularities are violated, no natural averages falsified, no natural actions perceptibly supplemented by his creative work.

Love Almighty and Ills Unlimited, pp. 98, 99

Prayer as God's Action in Us

It was an old-world maxim that heaven should be prayed to give us what we could not give ourselves. What lay within our scope was up to us. It would be mere laziness to pray for virtue or for peace of mind; one should go and cultivate them.

It is plain that on this basis prayer has no future. We do not think that what is outside our control should be prayed for; we think it should be brought under our control.

Where, then, does prayer find its place? Not in the supplementing of our efforts by magical invocations but in the very creation of our efforts. Prayer is the practical expression from our side of the conviction that the Creator works by making his creatures make themselves. Sub-rational creatures cannot have religion because they cannot participate voluntarily in the Creator's work. We can do this, and therefore we pray. That maxim of the old pagan world excluded what is most intimately and inviolably 'I' from the matter of my prayer. According to our view of things, what is most 'I' or 'mine' is the live point of prayer. It is a paradox of language, but a commonplace of experience, that a man is never so truly himself as when his action is God's. 'The more truly it is God, the more truly it is I.' That is where God and man come together.

The Brink of Mystery, p. 126

PENTECOST 20

===

Marriage and Love-Affairs

To go on steadily in a tranquil and loving obedience to God. But how? Perhaps - if I dare suggest to you anying so unromantic - we may get some light on the matter by observing the difference between steady marriages and exciting love-affairs.

The difference to which I will call attention is a difference in the expression of the positive emotion. In love-affairs, it tends to get expressed in common pleasures; in marriage, rather in common enterprises. When the pleasures are over, they are over, and leave the field clear for a reaction. But the common enterprises reach away into the future, and continue to unite us in the pursuit of them. The revolving day brings round its tasks unbidden; common cares mutually endear us, when common delights would only exhaust us.

So, then, the worship of the heart is a fine thing, and it would be wretched if we could never delight in God, or enjoy our religion. But our piety must grow into set customs, continuous enterprises in union with God's grace. If in our worship we can dwell with affection on God's goodness, or in prayer on the names of our fellow men, how excellent. But we must form resolutions. Lord, what wilt thou have me to *do*? What does my neighbour need from me? There is no need for resolutions to be original since we are so bad at keeping them. All we often need is to revive them. What they *must* be, is practical and particular: to pray at the hour I had promised, to be at communion on Sunday, to visit the sick friend, to answer the awkward correspondent, not to let so-and-so provoke me, to keep proper hours for my work, to avoid my besetting sin.

And we must examine ourselves when we pray, whether we have done what we promised.

The End of Man, pp. 171, 172

Faithfulness and Personal Identity

Faithfulness, then, is the thing which most forcibly convinces us of personal identity. If we rely on a friend's words, we know that he will not become a different person; for if he did, he might change his mind and let us down. He may become a different person in many ways; he may change his tastes and occupations, many of his opinions; but he will not become a different person in this particular way; not, that is, in respect of his faithfulness to me.

We commonly say that those who have no faithfulness have no character, no constancy of person at all; they seem to hang together by the mere fact of attachment to a single body; that body being destroyed, what is there, what thread of real being, on which God can bestow a share of his own immortal life?

Let us think now of the childish token, the card of resolutions we signed at our confirmation . . . Since then we have changed in so many ways; I do not think now as I thought then; I behave in many ways differently . . . But being faithful to God is still the same endeavour; the thoughts which lie behind those old written resolves and heart-searchings show us in the same posture before God as we stand in today. The same words will serve us, the same motions of the heart. This part of us is permanent, this is the immortal soul in us, for this is our fidelity to our faithful God, to him who changes not.

Religion is not self-improvement, or decent conduct or emotional worship. Religion is fidelity. 'Promise unto the Lord your God and keep it', says the psalm. But the fidelity which is the soul of religion is not our fidelity, it is God's. We give ourselves to him in no reliance on our own trustworthiness. Experience has taught us what we are. Our confidence is that God's faithfulness will prevail over our faithlessness, that he will recall us, that he will not let us go. Our broken resolutions witness against us, but he renews to us daily the miracle of his forgiveness, because he is faithful to his friends.

Said or Sung, pp. 160, 161, 162, 163

The Steady Current

When Christ was hanging on the cross on a spring afternoon, we may be certain that the most conscious part of his human mind was so ravaged by the pain he suffered, that he could think very little of other things. Yet the Eternal Father who knows all things saw these inescapable agonies as accidents and distractions. Underneath he saw the current of Christ's will steadily running in its set direction. He knew that he was praying for the salvation of mankind with the whole weight of his sacrifice. With us it is very commonly different; our prayer occupies the surface of our mind, the main current of our will flows on underneath in the direction of our usual vanities. The prayer which saves the world is one with the existence of the man who prays. It is with such a prayer that the saints and Christ himself pray for men's happiness, prosperity and peace, and by the virtue of this sacrament our prayer and theirs is one.

The Crown of the Year, p. 32

I Will Not Let Thee Go

Religion is the service of God, faith is cleaving to God. God cannot be served, cannot be cleaved to, except for his own sake and because he is God. There is no advertisement for faith, no commendation of faith, but this testimony: we know that we have run away from God in vain, have forgotten him in vain, have delayed our repentances in vain. But we have been pulled back, made to remember, forced to repent, by our natural master, in whose service our true being lies.

Almighty God is pleased to wrestle with us gently, as he did with Jacob in the old Hebrew tale. And when we are young (and often afterwards) we twist and turn, and try to put him off. But, he says to us, 'a thousand veils may hide me, and yet I am here. Everything you think of me is false, but you know that, whatever I am, you have me to wrestle with.'

The evidence of faith (I talk of what I think I know) is the evidence of Almighty Power, to break and heal the will. And if we want to put it to the test, this is required of us: not to run away from God, but to face him and hold back the curtains of insincerity with steady hands, begging him for the truth about himself and us. And we shall come to know that whatever is a dream, this which takes hold of us is not a dream. Those who believe are those who cannot but believe.

If we are too lazy to pray for a matter of minutes before we go to breakfast, too careless or too mean to buy an alarm clock that we may be sure to rise and receive the sacrament well-prepared one day in seven, we are scarcely treating our religion with the seriousness of grown men, not to say our God with the honour due to a creator. Nor are we exposing our wills sufficiently to the grasp which must master them. I will not let thee go, says Jacob, except thou bless me: and how willing that mysterious wrestler is to bless. It is not on him we practise mastery, but on ourselves, when we say, I will not let thee go.

The End of Man, pp. 59, 60, 61

PENTECOST 21

Theme of the Week: The Christian Hope

———

Endless Godhead Endlessly Possessed

The most insidious error of our severe philosophical theologians is to set aside the life to come as a thing indifferent, a matter of no concern, which Christians may or may not believe. What? Do we see God in this life? Is it a matter of no concern, a thing indifferent, whether we are ever to attain our only end? If it is indifferent to our earth-bound thoughts, is it indifferent to the heart of God? They think too meanly of his love to us who call this hope in question. Belief in this infinite and invaluable gift, this partaking of God's eternity, is the acid test of genuine faith. Leave this out of account, and you can equivocate for ever on God's very existence: your talk about God can always be talk about the backside of nature, dressed in emotional rhetoric. But a God who reverses nature, a God who undoes death, that those in whom the likeness of his glory has faintly and fitfully shone may be drawn everlastingly into the heart of light, and know him as he is: this is a God indeed, a God Almighty, a God to be trusted, loved, adored.

The end of man is endless Godhead endlessly possessed, but that end flows back in glory on our mortal days, and gives a hope and meaning to whatever Christians do for love of God or love of one another. For we are all heirs of everlastingness, and whatever we do or are furnishes material to the hands which out of perishing stuff create eternal joy.

The End of Man, p. 4

165

No Other Consolation

The old women like to say that what happened was all for the best. They are probably wrong. Good, even animal good, such as physical health or a moderate plenty, is a more fertile breeder of good on the whole - yes, even of moral good - than distress of any kind can be. Were it otherwise, we should be faced with an intolerable dilemma. We should be bound to fear that in consulting our friends' natural happiness, we should be imperilling their spiritual salvation. Like certain truly fiendish monastic superiors and novice-masters, we should feel called upon to arrange artificial mortifications for our juniors, and to twist the tails of our fellow creatures for the good of their souls.

Good breeds more good than any evil can. It is a special revelation of God's divine power that he is able to bring some good even out of evil. But his use of evil for good ends does not immediately sterilize it; it continues to breed after its own kind. What perhaps most offends us in the old women's talk is a suggestion implied, rather than stated; the suggestion that the evil they deplore finds its characteristic or dominant effect in the redeeming feature they fix upon. The boy's motor-cycle slipped, and he was smashed against the wall. The effect of the bereavement on his father's heart may have been truly edifying; from a besotted, possessive parent he changed into a general philanthropist. But it is almost indecent to mention the fact; still more, to dwell upon it with any satisfaction. Who cares about the old man, anyway? He has had his life. The young man, alas! was cut off in his prime. His promise was unfulfilled; he never married the girl who loved him; he had no posterity. Nothing that happened to his father can make any difference to so absolute an evil.

Of all consolations the most glib and the most indecent in the ears of unbelievers is the promise of an invisible and an eternal good.

And yet there is no other consolation but this which carries any force. The issue is all or nothing; either we believe, or we do not. The half-believing moralities of the old women fall flat, so long as they equivocate on this single point. Has the boy perished as though he had never been, and is his father to go the same way in a few years? Then how trivial it is that the old man should sublimate his disappointed parenthood in an enthusiasm for the reclamation of young gangsters! He has begun his charitable work somewhat late in life; it is not to be thought that he will make much of a showing at it. But once admit that the characters of the tragedy are immortal souls, and the balance alters. The boy's premature death, though an undoubted flaw in the order of nature, and a wound in the body of human affection, is not so blank a loss as to make the mention of redeeming consequences an indecency; while the opening of the father's narrow heart, being the preparation of a soul for glory and a beginning of heaven on earth, obtains a weight which may fairly tell in the scale of compensations. Even the old man's ill-practised philanthropy begins to have an incalculable radiation. He may not appear an effective agent in his chosen work, but divine charity once lighted in him will kindle his fellow-workers, or awake a response somewhere. And all charity, visible or invisible to human eyes, is everlasting life.

Love Almighty and Ills Unlimited, pp. 177, 178, 179, 180

The Stuff of Heaven

Heaven, then, is a created sphere where God bestows his presence by his action, especially his action through heart and mind. And where is heaven? When I was a lad it was still supposed to be an insoluble problem. If heaven is completely non-spatial, then (we used to say) the heavenly life must be a featureless sea of feeling, a shapeless ecstasy; or anyhow, nothing you could fairly call the resurrection-state of man. Whereas if heaven has any form of spatial dimension, then it falls somewhere in the field of space; a telescope might record it, an astronaut might reach it. And so heaven is pulled back into the perishable universe.

A pretty puzzle, and I was amazed to hear it solemnly restated the other day by a professor of philosophy; for I had supposed that Einstein had shown it up once for all as a piece of nonsense. According to his unanswerable reasoning, space is not an infinite pre-existent field or area in which bits of matter float about. Space is a web of interactions between material energies which form a system by thus interacting. Unless the beings or energies of which heaven is composed are of a sort to interact physically with the energies in our physical world, heaven can be as dimensional as it likes, without ever getting pulled into our spatial field, or having any possible contact with us of any physical kind. There may well be contacts which are not physical at all between earthly minds and heavenly minds, but that's another story. How I wish we could explain the Einsteinian theory to St Augustine! Obviously his heaven is dimensional; but the stuff of glory which composes its constituents is surely not apt to interact with sticks and stones, with flesh and blood.

Think what we may of heavenly dimensions, heaven is a sphere of created being, where God bestows his presence. And this he does at least in three ways: by a more visible providence, making the whole order of things the evident expression of an infinite goodness; by a more abundant grace, making the minds of his people transparent to his thought and their hearts to his love; by an incarnate presence with them in the glorified man, Jesus Christ.

Saving Belief, pp. 144, 145

PENTECOST 22

Theme of the Week: The Two Ways

———

Face to Face

In former times what struck men about the Day of Judgement was that it would forbid men to get away with their crimes, but what may strike us about it, is that it will make us acknowledge our follies. Then we shall see face to face that supreme Good, which day by day and year by year we have neglected for toys and trifles. And the more we read in his eyes the light of mercy, the more grounds we shall have to condemn our own perversity, for having turned our backs day by day, and hour by hour, on so kind a Creator.

The End of Man, p. 41

A Real Danger

First, the teaching of Christ, the nature of our free will, and the way God deals with us all point in one direction: the loss of heaven is a real danger. Second, I observe that Christ teaches one thing with particular insistence. Men whose moral misery is disguised from them by comfort, pride or success, will find themselves after death a prey to that flame which can surely be nothing but the scorching truth. Third, I see that Christ speaks of the flame as everlasting, as a torment which does not lose its force, or die down. The sinner will vainly wait for it to exhaust itself, or hope to escape from it on to the further side. But I do not see that I am forbidden to ask, what then? Cannot everlasting Mercy save from everlasting fire, or let the irreconcilable perish in it?

The fate of ultimate impenitence is a mystery into which I am reluctant to look. If it overtakes any, I pray they may be few. But looking to myself, and the hopes a Christian dares to entertain, I find conscience and moral reason join forces with Catholic teaching, and forbid me to claim exemption from the burning of that flame.

Saving Belief, pp. 153, 154

169

The Pearl of Great Price

The Kingdom of Heaven, he says, is like a merchant man - and when Christ says 'the kingdom of heaven', as often as not he means 'the Royal Majesty of God' or, more simply, 'the Divine King'. God the King, then, is like a merchant man. But if so, what is the pearl? Look at the other parables with which the evangelist aligns this, and you will see. God is a peasant, who wants a crop, and he does not mind how much of the seed miscarries, as long as there is a harvest. God is a fisherman, who wants a catch: he does not mind how much rubbish comes in the net, as long as there are fish worth picking out. He is a shepherd, who will leave his flock to fend for itself, while he drags after the one lost sheep. He is a merchant man, who has set his heart on one pearl of great price, and thinks everything well lost, to gain it. So what is the pearl of price?

You are the pearl of price. A loyal and obedient heart is what the King of Heaven thinks the world well lost to win, and since he puts such a price on our souls, he has the best right to bid us not to undervalue them.

The parable of the pearl, then, describes the King of Heaven's quest for us, not our quest for him. And yet it is not perverse to take it the other way round as well. For we cannot go wrong, to imitate God. And if he sets an infinite value on the image of his face where it is shaped in us in mortal clay, we cannot go wrong, to value it in its heavenly original, or to love that Son, in whom the Father's heart supremely delights.

There result from what we have been saying two very simple truths. God is priceless to us, for what he is makes him so. We are priceless to God, for his kindness makes us so. Why then should I remember God, and serve God, day and night? Because he is all that is worth having to me; and because I am infinitely desired by his love. It needed no Christ to teach us that God is our sole and everlasting Good could we but attain him: what Christ showed us was that God desires us with all the love of his infinite heart.

The End of Man, pp. 42, 43

LAST SUNDAY AFTER PENTECOST

Theme of the Week: Citizens of Heaven

===

What Heaven to Be in Heaven

Ah, when shall love so clear my eyes, that I shall even see one half of what God has put into my neighbour, for me to love? - let alone care for him with the heart of God. Then what heaven, to be in heaven, and see on every side the glory of God reflected in the image of God, which is the human face! What heaven to be in heaven, and to delight, without a barrier, in the company of a thousand friends: when all reserves are down, and all hearts open, and we shall care for the handiwork of God impartially, whether it happens to be in another, or in ourselves!

The End of Man, p. 88

A Foretaste in This Life

It is silly to say, 'How marvellous to be in heaven! Our shirts will be whiter than the latest detergent can wash them, and we shall have no need to switch on the electric light.' It is not silly to say, 'Every now and then, perhaps, I manage to be at the disposal of God's will. How marvellous to be in heaven! I shall live in it all the time.' Nor is it silly to say, 'From time to time I think I catch a glimpse of what God is doing. How marvellous to be in heaven! I shall see his purposes in everything, as clearly as I read my friends' feelings on their faces.' Nor is it silly to say, 'Every now and then I see a bit of what God has put into the people round me. How marvellous to be in heaven! I shall see it all.' Nor is it silly to say, 'I acknowledge Christ by faith, and bless him in words for being very God and very man. How marvellous to be in heaven! I shall be familiar with the man in whom the Godhead is.'

If you consider the marvels I have mentioned, you will notice three things that are true of them all. First, they are joys of which we have a foretaste in this life; and so we know what we are talking about when we mention them. Second, they are joys which arise from a more perfect relation with realities- with God and with the children of God. Third, they are joys which might be actualized (for anything we know) under a variety of conditions, or states of being. Our faith in heaven is a confidence in the pattern of perfect relations; as for the state of being, we can leave it to God.

Saving Belief, p. 143

Beginning Again

This life is always a beginning, no more - and therefore it's heaven or nothing for us. But again - for the same reason, because of the infinity of God - heaven itself is always a beginning: a beginning, indeed, which for those that are there has really and firmly begun: the exploration of a Paradise of which more will always be before us than what we have seen. So that the loveliness we have known always increases our desire for the delight to which it points and leads us on; as we walk the way we are drawn into the very thought and action of God. We sing all too Jewishly of heaven, as a perpetual Sabbath: but the Sabbath was the seventh day; the closure of the week. Shall not we call heaven Sunday, an endless beginning, ceaseless wonder, perpetual resurrection in the unexhausted power of him who everlastingly makes all things new? Be sure of this, there is no coming to the end of God; the more we know of him and his ways, the more avenues will open for further exploration, or revelation, rather: we may explore God's creatures, but God is known as he bestows himself.

To return to earth - it's the end of the Church's year, and we may well do some self-examination and see how we have spent our time and how we have served our Creator. We shall find that all is to be begun again - who can say we have advanced? But we must be patient. God shapes us by his providence and by our very failures, if we will keep looking to him. He knows that the beginnings he has made with us are not in vain. For it is his good pleasure to give us the Kingdom.

A Celebration of Faith, p. 165

FESTIVALS AND HOLY DAYS

The Naming of Jesus, or the Circumcision of Christ

1 January

If we are speaking of the scriptural signs, the providential configurations of the sacred text, most striking of all, perhaps, is that which (if we are to believe St Justin) most moved the Jew with whom he disputed: I mean the position of the name of Jesus in the Old Testament. The matter is disguised from us by the use of Joshua in the Old Testament and Jesus in the New. But the names are one. Assimilate them, and what do you find? How is it that these words came to stand in the prophecy of Zechariah? 'The angel said, Be silent, all flesh, before the Lord, for he is waked up out of his holy habitation. And he showed me Jesus the great Priest standing before the Angel of the Lord, and Satan standing at his right hand to be his adversary.' Then, in the sequel, Jesus is justified and Satan condemned, and this is the salvation of all Israel. Or again, lower down in the same prophecy, 'Make crowns and set them on the head of Jesus . . .' No less wonderful are the significations that hang about the earlier Jesus, the son of Nun, whom we call Joshua, and after whom, presumably, our Saviour was principally named. For how surprising it is that Moses, the patron and the glory of the ancient law, was unable to fulfil his own work, or to bring the people to inherit the promises of God, but was obliged to leave all fulfilment and all victory to a successor, and that successor no other than Jesus. Moreover, this Jesus alone of Old Testament heroes is associated with the cross. For of him alone it is recorded that he crucified the potentates he overthrew. And this prompts St Paul, applying the principle of the *coincidentia oppositorum*, to reflect that the greater Jesus, by himself willingly accepting crucifixion, crucified the hostile powers in his own flesh. The bond that was against us, he says, he abolished, nailing it to the cross; he put off as a garment the principalities and powers, and publicly gibbeted them, triumphing over them on the tree. These surprising significations which follow the name of Jesus are not evidences, but signs only; but they are wonderful none the less, and they are the providences of God.

Interpretation and Belief, pp. 30, 31

The Conversion of St Paul

23 January

Since St Paul wears his heart on his sleeve, perhaps it is no impertinence on our part to say that pride was his besetting temptation. Of course his pride was not of the childish sort which is out for status and outward dignity. That sort of pride would not have led him to stitch tents in Aquila's shop, rather than draw an apostle's salary. No, his pride was of an altogether subtler sort; he would rather give than receive. He saw himself as a sort of universal father, providing for his spiritual children. And of course it was true: that's what he was. And at the same time he did learn to take. He saw that he couldn't carry on his mission without his disciples' friendship and prayers. And when he was old, and helpless, and in prison, it was his friends' turn to give, and his to receive. It was all one life they had together in Christ: now it flowed this way, now it flowed that way; whichever way the current of giving went, it was a common happiness.

The End of Man, pp. 44, 45

Timothy and Titus

26 January

We will begin by listing a few principles:

1 To hope for heaven has nothing particularly selfish about it. No one ever thought he could keep heaven to himself.
2 Heaven is not a cash payment for walking with God; it's where the road goes.
3 Heaven isn't an optional extra; our belief is nonsense without it.
4 Our reason for believing it isn't that nature points to it, but that it leads us to itself.

I should like to develop the last point a bit. Heaven is nothing that created nature produces; it is a new creation. Two consequences follow from this. The first is, that we have no interest in trying to isolate a piece of us called soul, which tends to outlive the body's collapse. Our immortality is the new gift of God, not the survival of our old nature, whether in whole or in part. It was pagan Greeks who talked about immortal soul, and with reason; for (to put it shortly) they thought the human spirit was a piece of godhead, able to guarantee immortal being to itself. The religion of the Bible teaches no such doctrine. God alone can give us a future. It is better, then, to talk about the resurrection of man than about the immortality of soul. Belief in resurrection is belief not in ourselves, but in God who raises us. It is in fact the acid test, whether we believe in God or not. A God who raises the dead is a real power; he is not just a fanciful name for the order of nature, whether physical or moral.

Saving Belief, pp. 140, 141

The Presentation of Christ in the Temple

2 February

Mary was most blessed, because for her the natural love of parenthood could run on unbroken into the love of that Son whom God had supernaturally given. And so Christians have desired to have her prayers, not because special virtues are recorded of her, but because she has a path of incomparable simplicity into the heart of God's love. In company with her, we too have desired to find access; we have followed her through the stages of her journey. First, Jesus is in her arms, and has no life independently from her; she carries him to the temple, she presents him before God. Then, even in his childhood, he shows a mysterious life of his own. Now he walks into the temple on his own feet at his mother's side, and there detaches himself; he remains hearing the doctors, and asking them questions. She misses him, and seeks him sorrowing; she finds him about a business of his own, or of his heavenly Father's (it is all one) in his Father's house. Now he is something that she has not made him, his heart and mind are not under her hand; yet he returns to Nazareth, and is subject to her, for he is a child still. The day comes when he is no longer subject, but she is subjected to him: 'Whatsoever he bids,' she said to the servants at Cana, 'do it.' And so, from a mother, she came to be a worshipper; she lived in him – not in what she made him, but in what he made of her.

How blest was she, above all women; and how happy are we, if, following her progress with devout imagination, we can come to live, even for the short period of our prayer, in that Son whom God has given to us, caring for his concerns, and not for ours! For what else is it to pray, but this: that we live for a little while in the Son of God, and share in some measure the love he has for all the men with whom we have to do? That we deeply care for the fulfilment in them of his saving work, and worthily prize the work of his mercy in our own souls?

Said or Sung, pp. 28, 29

179

St Joseph of Nazareth, Husband of the Blessed Virgin Mary

19 March

By sitting late over Greek print in a badly lighted library, I finished my eyes and Schools together. I was forbidden to read for three months. Not read for three months? What was I to do? 'Look,' said my father, 'the fence round the garden is falling to pieces, we'll replace it. We'll do it in oak; and we won't buy the uprights ready slotted, we'll cut them out with hand tools.' So we made that solid oak paling right round the garden, my father and I. I wonder whether it still stands? The weeks flew by, the long sunshiny days of satisfying manual labour. I never had a happier summer than that summer I was supposed to be blind. There was the pleasure of doing a great work, and overcoming hourly difficulties. But above all, there was the pleasure of working with my father, who did not make himself the boss – he accepted me as an equal. All the time there was the feeling of his kindness, who had undertaken such a labour to keep me cheerful; but there was nothing indebting in it, it was so obvious he enjoyed the work as much as I did. My zest, however great, could not equal his.

Do you ever write to your fathers? It is an amiable and can even be an enjoyable exercise. There is a special reason. God has made known to us the mysteries of his kindness through human parables. But what makes these parables so forcible, is that they are not merely parables we can grasp, but parables we must enact. That is why they get right in amongst us. He has given us the friendship of Father and Son, on a level of equality – *nihil in hoc Trinitate vel maius vel minus* – as the clue to the most august of mysteries, the life of the Godhead. It is hard for us to worship the divine reality, if we are falsifying in our own person the human parable: if we are ungrateful or indifferent sons to our earthly fathers. I am so sorry for those of you who have to try to be otherwise; I never had to try at all. My little blind soul, nosing its way into the world, had been so careful in the choice of a father.

The End of Man, pp. 67, 68, 69

The Annunciation of our Lord to the Blessed Virgin Mary

25 March

Like sunlight in a burning-glass, God's love for us all narrows to a needle of fire, and pierces Mary at Gabriel's salutation. Her young heart quivers at the touch, and, when she has reconciled herself to God's grace, still does not know what it will lay on her. When she declares herself the handmaid of the Lord, she enslaves herself to the service of an invisible point which begins from that moment to be in her; a point of infinite growing-power, our joy, our love, our immortality, God Only-Begotten.

Lord I Believe, p. 88

St Mark the Evangelist

25 April

Shall we reduce St Mark's Gospel to three lines?

> God gives you everything.
> Give everything to God.
> You can't.

True, there is a fourth line; Christ will make you able, for he has risen from the dead. But this is almost overshadowed in St Mark's Gospel by the emphasis on self-distrust. St Mark seems even more afraid that his readers will trust themselves than that they will distrust Christ's risen power.

Well, perhaps the Mark of the Gospel was the John Mark of Acts, after all. And perhaps all this emphasis on desertion, running away, the failure of good intentions has something to do with that most painful text in the Book of Acts: 'Barnabas wished to take John called Mark with them; but Paul thought it not well to take with them him who had turned back from them in Pamphylia, and not gone with them to the work.' If the Evangelist is that Mark who had once turned back, and of whom St Paul had thought the worse for his turning back, then he had evidently learned from his turning back what God wished him to learn from it: that it is not in us to follow Christ, it is Christ's gift.

God has given you much; you have not given anything worth mentioning to God. Well, St Mark (if he is indeed the same man) went back from the work in Pamphylia, and in Gethsemane none of the disciples behaved with credit. It is by these desolating experiences that God teaches us to trust him, not ourselves. The more emptied out you are, the more hope there is of your learning to be a Christian. Now is the very moment – there will never be a better – for you to put your trust in the God who makes something from nothing, who raises the dead.

Said or Sung, pp. 98, 99

St Philip and St James, Apostles

1 May

The sun, in the height of a clear moon, radiates on every earthly thing that lies open to his light; and so a transcendent Godhead must radiate on every creature subject to his will. All things are external to his being; nothing is outside the sphere of his action . . . It is physically impossible for anything to exist in the sun's region of space, and not be linked with him by a line of living light. There is no such thing as mere coexistence between the sun and any element of his environment; there is always a live relation, an instantaneous flow of fire. And similarly, though nature is created to act of her own motion, there is no such thing as the mere coexistence of any part of her with the being of God. If anything exists, the divine Goodness radiates upon it.

Are you brave enough to believe in God at all? If you are, you are bound to digest this bewildering fact: God cannot be God, he cannot differ from us in the essential way which makes us finite and him infinite, unless his mind is infinite too; and an infinite mind cannot conceivably be liable to preoccupation. For us men, attending to one thing means disattending from another. The universe queues up for its turn of our attention, and most of it will go home disappointed, like nine thousand in a crowd of ten thousand who thought they would shake hands with the Queen. The Queen has only two hands, and she is not expected to shake with more than one of them. We have a restricted power of attention, or of thought, and we do well if we bring the half of it to bear most of the time. But God is God; he is a being and a life infinite or unlimited; he can and does give an entire, an adequate and an undivided attention to every single creature and every single circumstance.

Saving Belief, pp. 43, 44, 45

St Matthias the Apostle

14 May

Poor Matthias, unlucky saint! We shall always think of you as the man who isn't Judas; there is no other circumstance of your life, good or bad, on record, except your having been substituted for that apostate soul . . .

One could preach, indeed, for several hours on the significance of Matthias's election: the fact that, when one of the twelve went to hell (as they supposed) his colleagues found another in his place; whereas, when one of them went to heaven by the most sure road of martyrdom, they did not dream of replacing him. Here is much food for thought. Evidently, to start with, heaven and earth were all one thing to those heaven-centred minds. The Church, the Israel of God, must be complete, an army brigaded, like the old Israel, under twelve patriarchs or princes. When Christ chose twelve disciples, he did not act by chance; he was making it plain for all to see, that God's twelvefold Israel was being rebuilt on new foundations. The twelve foundations, the twelve apostles, must remain. If one fell into the abyss, he must be replaced; if one was raised to glory, he was all the more confirmed in his apostleship: for he was with Christ, and Christ was the very heart and substance of the Church, whether on earth or in heaven.

The End of Man, p. 116

The Visit of the Blessed Virgin Mary to Elizabeth

31 May

God reaches out to God. God's miracle in Mary carries her to visit her cousin, whom he has blessed already with a kindred mercy. She goes, and our salvation travels with her; the secret of incarnate God is folded in her womb. She may seem to carry him where she pleases; but no one takes God anywhere who is not sent by Almighty Wisdom. The going is in Mary's feet, but God directs her heart, and God is the blessing she brings. She arrives, and the grace in her joins hands with the grace in Elizabeth; at the sound of Mary's greeting the child of promise leaps in her cousin's womb.

Lord I Believe, p. 88

St Barnabas the Apostle

11 June

Is not this strange, that God should be found in our handiwork rather than in his own; in our little heaps of stones rather than in his mighty mountains? And yet, if we think of it, it is not so strange after all. For what we look for when we look for a shrine, a temple, or an altar, is not simply the presence of our Almighty Creator. What we look for is a place where he is at home with us. When Jacob fled from Esau through strange wildernesses, he did not need to be convinced of God's general power. God's terrible world was all around him in the wind and the rocks and the open glittering sky. What he needed to know, poor man, was that God would come and be at home with him.

If God accepts to dwell in what we have built, then he is ours, he is at home with men; and so men have been always forward to build temples, altars, shrines, that they might have God to be with them.

That is it, then. Here in St Barnabas's Church, in the place that men have built and dedicated, God desires to be at home with you. He is not content to be the God of the world, or to be the God of highest heaven, he must also be your God and inhabit where you have built. Now everything that God desires he desires with the whole of his heart. God has not got a mere corner of his heart for this corner of the world which is called St Barnabas's parish, for that is not what God is like. God's caring for one thing does not get in the way of his caring for another thing: all the world is in his heart, yet he loves every part of it with all his heart. He desires to dwell in every corner and cranny of his creation, and his whole heart is in every such desire. We never have to do with a part of God, with so much of God as God can spare us: we just have to do with God. God is whole, and God is one, and his heart is set on dwelling with you here, and being at home with you here.

The End of Man, pp. 164, 165, 166, 167

The Birth of St John the Baptist

24 June

Perhaps the chief mark of sanctity is an attitude of utter simplicity in face of the divine will, and the divine promises. Such was the attitude of Christ himself.

We think of seriousness as something which needs to be forced, or put on. Whereas to genuine faith, seriousness is just naked simplicity; it is non-hypocrisy, non-evasiveness, non-sophistication, in face of the normal environment of the believing soul, which is the ever-present will of God. To be serious, you have only to open your eyes; a man driving on a mountain road does not relax attention to the hairpin bends, and a Christian finding his way in the will of God does not lose sight of the way-marks.

Sanctity is never out of date; and sanctity is nothing but entire simplicity towards God.

The Brink of Mystery, pp. 153, 154

St Peter the Apostle

or

St Peter and St Paul, Apostles

29 June

The spirit of faction, and of that self-hatred which is the twin of self-righteousness, can so bedevil religion as to make it a form of positive evil, and a blinding of the heart. Where is the man who will see things as they are and allow God to instruct his mind through an unbiased appreciation? He is the man without an axe to grind; and the first thing the world sees in religious believers, is that they are the grinders of axes. They dare not take things as they come, or see things as they are, for fear of disturbing their prejudices or cherished beliefs.

Who can say, surveying the field of history, whether religion, yea, and even professed Christianity, has been a greater cause of blindness and rancour than of charity and vision? I do not think the historical case is worth fighting. But then spiritual truth was never known by counting heads: the saints are our instructors. And it is still true, that the best way to see and love the work of God in all this world of his is to look for it, and when we see it, to adore. And this, true religion does.

A Celebration of Faith, p. 196

St Thomas the Apostle

3 July

St Thomas told no lies. He believed some things, but he did not, at that time, believe Christ's resurrection. Then Christ gave him his body to be the proof: and he gives us his body to be the proof. Christ's body is still in the world, his body is his faithful people. It was not every part of Christ's body that equally convinced St Thomas, it was the parts that carried the prints of the crucifixion. And it is not every part of Christ's body now that convinces us, it is the crucified parts: not every member of Christ, not every common Cristian, but the saints who are marked with the signs of Christ's sacrifice. There are such men in the world, and we have known them: men whose words are like their faces and their faces like their hearts, and their hearts printed with the cross of Jesus. Jesus made them what they are, his death and resurrection is manifest in them. We have known them, let us not forget them: and may he who taught St Thomas take hold of our groping hands, and guide them to the prints of his saving wounds, where they can be seen and felt in the lives of Christ's true servants and saints; that in them we may acknowledge and glorify him who alone is worthy of all glory.

The End of Man, pp. 19, 20

St Mary Magdalen

22 July

To meet God, it is not enough that we should die. God, out of his invisible omnipresence, must gather himself to meet us in a form we can recognize. And how he will do this, Christians are not left to conjecture; they know. God revealed himself in the human body of Jesus, and in that same person he will visit us again. But in what form, through the pages of gospel story, does the Godhead already stand revealed?

Christ shone in his transfiguration, but it was a single episode, and it was not the basis of the gospel. The divine life which radiated through him took effect in words, deeds and sufferings; a saving action developed in discourse, and in mutual dealing with friends or enemies; more especially with friends. The Christ of the Gospels can only be known through what he did, and in the doing of it. And how shall the Christ of Advent be known, but through what he has done, and the possession of it? If Christ's glory and Godhead were at first manifest in his saving of men, and in the men he saved, how shall these things be manifest at last, but in the men he has saved, and in their being at one with him?

Love Almighty and Ills Unlimited, pp. 128, 129

St James the Apostle

25 July

I have heard that a Christian soul, released from the flesh, was shown a shining crown high above, and told to fly upwards to it. But on nearer approach, what had seemed a wreath for the head appeared now as a wide circle of light, such as we sometimes admire in the clouds round the moon. Still more nearly seen, the clouds were revealed as hosts of heavenly witnesses, blessed saints, on whom rays from the centre broke, and were reflected in the form of a shining crown. The newcomer thought with relief: 'After all, I do not have to wear this crown; I may lose myself among the myriads who make it up.' He dropped into his place among old friends, and was at peace. But he was no sooner there than his mind slipped away from him, and flew into the heart of that glory which sat throned in the midst, a glory in whose body there were five wounds, like sunspots in the body of the sun. United with the centre from which all love goes forth, and to which all love returns, he felt the whole wreath of light, the company of the saints, pressing round him; and so he wore the crown, the crown of which he was himself a part, and which no cross of his had merited.

We are all called to be saints: our place on high is appointed, and there is no reward short of union with the heart of Christ. God has only one thing to give: he gives himself. We cannot aim lower.

Said or Sung, p. 26

The Transfiguration of our Lord

6 August

Jesus, the healer and teacher of multitudes, turns his face to Jerusalem and death. Before he goes, he climbs high into the hills. He prays, and the cloud touches him. He is transfigured, and what he is, shines out of him. Old saints are visible in his light, conversing with him. It is good to be here; if good for Peter and his companions, how much more blest for Christ, that he should inhabit a mountain hermitage, taken up in God. But men must be illuminated, and from another station; a wooden candlestick on Calvary awaits the light of the world.

Lord I Believe, p. 91

St Bartholomew the Apostle

24 August

In the everlastingness of future bliss the soul might travel far, and explore all societies, learning to praise God for the variety of his works; everywhere filled with eternity and under the direct shining of God's countenance, omnipresent as the sun where there is no night; yet everywhere discovering in societies of love the inexhaustibly various image of Christ, alive in them all. Some have been frightened by the dimension of everlastingness which heavenly promises imply; and yet only in infinite successive states and acts of blessed life, can we know and love the body of Christ, of which we are the living members.

Everlasting ages may bring us through the villages of Israel; but in this present life we shall not pass far beyond our own hamlet. Whether heaven is distributed in villages or combined in cities, the heaven of this present life, the fellowship of prayer, certainly has a village organization. With how few souls living or departed have we such an effective communion that we can really pray for them! And when we extend beyond those limits, and pray for the whole society of Christ's Church, it is not that our single prayers can move the mighty mass, but rather that we in our village of prayer reach out and touch the prayers of other villages, and make our act of faith in Christ, the master of all our prayers; Christ who is able to inspire all the villages of his people with the spirit of prayer, and so to unite their prayers in himself, that the whole estate of his Church is benefited and edified.

Said or Sung, pp. 135, 136

The Blessed Virgin Mary

8 September

Mysteries of Glory

Taking up

The bond of the incarnation is unbreakable, and Mary, dying, is united with her Son. He came from her womb, she goes into his mystical body; once she was home for him, now he is home to her. She surrenders to him the flesh from which he had his own. He takes up the pieces where she lays them down and remakes her life in the stuff of glory. He cherishes the dear familiar body, entirely her own in every part, and entirely the work of his hands.

Crown of Life

Mary is crowned with the diadem of life, her height of degree in the happy-making vision of God. When Simeon had feasted his eyes on God's salvation he was willing to depart, but what Mary sees will never let her go. For though God be Spirit and invisible to sense, he is perfectly known in infinite actions. No word, no gesture, no conduct ever betrayed love to love as God's heart is laid open in the whole state and life of heaven. His unveiled countenance is the whole face of things, and the eyes are Jesus Christ, God seeing and visible.

Before each mystery:
Our Father . . . but deliver us from evil. Amen.
With each mystery, ten times:
Hail Mary, full of grace, the Lord is with thee.
Blessed are thou among women
And blessed is the fruit of thy womb, Jesus.
Holy Mary, mother of God, pray for us sinners now and at the hour of our death. Amen.
After each mystery, once:
Glory be to the Father . . . without end. Amen.

Lord I Believe, p. 95

Holy Cross Day

14 September

For what did he do, but set about bringing men into union with his Father by association with himself? He did not wait to be crucified before he began the reconstitution of God's people round the standard of his empire. Under the actual conditions of human frailty and human revolt, the bringing of men into such a union was not completed without the death of Christ. It was not only that those who rebelled against their king crucified him; it was just as much that those who were pledged to him deserted him. What was it, though, that produced such tragic reactions, the murderous rebellion of some, with the accompanying desertion of others? What but the thing which would, we say, have been the work of Christ in any case, the initiation of the mystical union? He began extending the divine life and will outside his own person, to become the life of others by association; it was against this movement that rebellion was raised, and from this movement that desertion fell away.

It is often said that there is a tension, if not a contradiction, between two expressions of our faith, one in terms of incorporation with Christ's body, the other in terms of reconciliation through his death. The incorporation theology is sacramental and Catholic, the reconciliation theology is Protestant and personal. That Catholics and Protestants have quarrelled is as undeniable as it is tragic. But so far from there being a natural tension between incorporation and atonement, each needs the other and without the other neither makes sense. Christ did not come to get himself killed; he was not a suicide. He came to associate his people with divine life, and they killed him for doing this. By so dying he reconciled sinful wills to God, and made their incorporation in his mystical body a real possibility.

Saving Belief, pp. 112, 113

195

St Matthew the Apostle

21 September

There is no need to *argue* against the cult of Mammon: it only needs to be exposed. There is no need to *demonstrate* that money is a good servant, but a bad master. The truth is self-evident, and that would be the end of the matter if Mammon were lodged in our heads. Unfortunately it is not so: he is deeply entrenched in our hearts. 'Lay not up for yourself treasure upon earth,' says the voice of Truth himself, 'for where your treasure is, there will your heart be also.' And, 'No man can serve two masters – you cannot serve God and Mammon.' There is only one way to be rid of Mammon-worship, and that is to stop reckoning anything as our own. You cannot serve two masters. If God is the master, everything we have is his; money and the manipulation of money are instrumental to his will.

In the parables of pounds and talents, Christ compares God with a master who entrusted money to his servants, and then called them to account for their management of it. It is commonly supposed that the money of the parable is just a figure of speech. What God essentially requires an account of from us is our use of our gifts and graces: our talents in the metaphorical sense. It is not at all clear to me that this is so – no doubt the parable has a wider application, as wide, indeed, as you can make it – but why should not the first and plainest sense be starkly literal? Will not God call us to account for what we have done with our money? And – one might almost say – the man who can pass that account need be subjected to no other, for what we have done with our money is what we have done with our life. The man who has made an imaginative, a generous, a just, a creative, a living use of his money is a perfect man.

The End of Man, p. 84

St Michael and All Angels

29 September

Why do we believe in the holy angels? What's the point of it? Well, obviously we believe in them on the word of Jesus Christ, on the testimony of saints and of the holy Church, and because it was an angel brought the tidings to Mary when she conceived by the Holy Ghost. But if you ask what is the principal part of the belief – why we are to suppose that God created angels – I shall reply that the puzzle isn't why God created angels, but why he ever created anything else. It does not puzzle me, that the sun in the sky surrounds himself with light, for it's his nature to shine in all directions; so why should it puzzle me that God surrounds himself with glorious angels, in whom his creative goodness is displayed? The sun shoots the same quality of light in all directions, up, down and round, but on this point the sun differs from God, who never sends out two rays of glory which are alike. His power is so various, that each of his creatures expresses it differently: Michael, Gabriel, Raphael, thousands on thousands of shining spirits, each serve and love God in their own unique way and reflect a different aspect of his infinite glory.

Why do we believe in angels? We start from what we can see, the glory of God in this mixed world of bright and dark. We say, this world of ours isn't the home of glory, glory comes from above; it descends, as St James says, from the Father of lights, in whom is no change nor shadow of alteration. We trace glory up to its home, and ask, how that home is furnished and populated? We reply, it is peopled with angels.

The End of Man, p. 32

197

St Luke the Evangelist

18 October

We think we shall see Christ in glory, who have been shown him in humility; and perhaps we think the glory will be an aureole of golden light, a stature above the human, the majesty of a voice like many waters. And no doubt the voice and countenance of Jesus express whatever can be expressed of human grace and majesty; but the blinding radiance, the physical tokens of Godhead, must surely be written off as the merest poetry. The Godhead of Christ is acknowledged by the perception that God acts through him and as he, making him the king and focus of the spiritual universe. And this is seen to be so, because all the saints turn to him and centre themselves upon him. The glory of Christ is not a radiation of physical light, reflected on a thousand faces; the glory of Christ is the love of Christ, to which a thousand thousand hearts respond. It is in the universal worship of the redeemed creation, that the Christhood of Jesus will be manifest to us.

And so the Father himself will be seen and known; not that any eye ever saw him, or can see. In heaven, as on earth, he will be manifest in his works; but his works will there be like music in the hands of a master, the mere utterance of his mind. The redeemed will be that living music, through their perfect response to his will. Each one will know God through the entire obedience of his own heart to God, God who works all his works in him. Yet how small a part will each one be alone in that great symphony of spiritual being which expresses the glory of God! All God's glory cannot be expressed, no, not by heaven itself; God is infinite, God is the abyss of being and of joy, and heaven itself is a kingdom made up of finite creatures. But all of God that can be expressed to such as we are, finds expression in the manifold societies of saints above.

The Brink of Mystery, pp. 50, 51

St Simon and St Jude, Apostles

28 October

It is easy to say, 'Be yourself', if you could find the self you are supposed to be: but what is it? Some people think that they are being themselves, and wonderfully sincere, if they identify themselves with their worst and most primitive passions. But that is to be little better than an animal, and how can I be myself by being a beast? I am a man, surely, and how can I be myself by forgetting my noblest part? Where is the sincerity in a man's being a beast? Yet if I attempt to follow a higher ideal of myself, how easily do I become a prig or a hypocrite.

The saint has solved the problem of sincerity in the sole possible way by turning to God, the great I AM, and accepting the self his creator designed for him. And the quest of the self God has meant each of us to be is like the quest of happiness (which is indeed much the same thing) - it is not found by looking for it. We do not ask of God, 'What sort of person did you mean me to be?' - we say to him 'Lord, what wilt thou have me to do?'

A Celebration of Faith, pp. 199, 200

All Saints' Day

1 November

The divine life came to earth in Jesus, he was the heart and centre of it: but the divine life could not live or act in Jesus alone. The divine life had to use his parents, his kindred and his friends, to make Jesus a man; and had to use his disciples and associates to keep him being a man; for we cannot go on being human, any more than we can get to be human, without other people.

Jesus was more of a man, not less of one, by having died and risen; he needs men not less, but more, if he is to continue his divinely human life; for now his range of fellowship is unlimited, he spreads himself over mankind.

It was only a matter of months, it seems, until Stephen followed Jesus, and died a martyr; then James – and Mary died, we do not known just when. And so the friends of Christ in Paradise built up to a great company, and meanwhile his friends on earth did not decrease but constantly added to their numbers. Still Jesus is only Jesus by what his friendship does in human souls, whether those souls are on earth or in heaven. In heaven – for naturally, those who are joined in one life and action with the Son of God cannot die. How should they die? As Jesus said to Martha, distressed for the death of her brother Lazarus, 'I am the Resurrection and the Life'.

A martyr is only a martyr because his sacrifice was the act of Christ in him, and a saint is only a saint because his life is the life of Christ in him. All the feast days of the saints are feast days of Christ – of the Christ in Francis or the Christ in Bernard or the Christ in Paul. They are what they are by feeding on Christ, just as we feed on Christ; having union with Christ in the Holy Sacrament we have union with all his people, all his mystical body.

And above all, the Feast of All Saints is a feast day of Jesus Christ, the feast of all his glorious actions in the whole body of the people he saves.

A Celebration of Faith, pp. 104, 105, 106

Commemoration of the Faithful Departed

2 November

If Dives needed to be stripped, and to suffer the truth of his condition, do not we also? Perhaps, before we suffer it, we may be assured of mercy; perhaps the sight of mercy will make the torment, when we see what a God we have, and how we have served him; what wounds we have inflicted on the souls of our fellows by our egotism and neglect.

Purgatory was rejected by our Reformers, as undermining the sufficiency of Christ's atonement; for it was taken to be the serving of a sentence by which the guilt of Christians was in some way worked off. Such an objection has no force against the teaching, that we have a pain to pass through, in being reconciled to truth and love. And we may as well call this pain purgatorial, having no other name to call it. It seems strange, indeed, that so practical and pressing a truth as that of purgatory should be dismissed, while so remote and impractical a doctrine as the absolute everlastingness of hell should be insisted on. Nor is it that ultimate fire is scriptural, while remedial fire is not. Remedial fire was taught plainly enough by St Paul to his Corinthians.

Saving Belief, pp. 154, 155

St Andrew the Apostle

30 November

If you ask me to remember the dead, to pray even for the dead, I am utterly bewildered. So many millions – my mind is numbed by the huge arithmetic of death. To gather and concentrate my thoughts, and yours, maybe I will tell the story of one man, than whom I never knew a better. He, at least, was all of one piece. He died, as you shall hear, because he did not care about himself: but then he never had cared about himself, since he grew up, and came to know what he was after. It was many years after the war that I named this man, being dead, to a fellow soldier. His face changed. There wasn't a man like that in the regiment, he said. He was sober and happy: and he didn't care whether he lived or died when we were in the thick of it. He used to say to us, as though we should all feel the same, 'Isn't it marvellous to think that any one of us might see the face of God tomorrow!'

He was killed. And why? He would not let his men advance, until he had made his personal reconnaissance, to be sure that there were no machine-gun posts left behind by the retreating enemy, and missed by Allied observation. Well, there was a machine-gun post; Hugh Lister was shot, and so his men were not taken by surprise.

I have told you the story of a heroic, hearty, enjoying sort of man, who just cared for the will of God, as other men care for the girl they love or, more likely, for themselves. I have told you the story, because, for all our pious professions, it is so easy to forget that the lovers of God really exist. We know we are supposed to love God, and we go through various exercises in the hope of doing it; the saints just do it. So many men *were* sacrificed in the war, but here was a man who made the oblation of himself with a willing heart, and scarcely knew that he did – his eyes were not on himself, they were turned elsewhere.

The Brink of Mystery, pp. 115, 118

St Stephen the First Martyr

26 December

I knew a man whose name, though uncanonized, I shall always silently mention when I recall at the altar of God those saints whose fellowship gives reality to our prayers; a man who sacrificed in the prime of his age a life which he had never lived for himself; a man whose eyes sparkled with all the passions, pity, indignation, sorrow, love, delight, but never for himself; unless it is more proper to say, Yes, for himself; since he had made God's lives and God's concerns his own, and had no others you would greatly notice.

Such a life, then, is evidence; and what other evidence could you hope to find? We have no inspection, no insight into the works of nature, which could conceivably let us through them to a vision of anything that lies beneath; all we can study is the diagram their movements draw in space. The only being we can know from within is our own; we are forced, however inadequate it may be, to take it as a sample of the rest, and judge the world from man. And man knows God only by yielding to him; we do not know the fountain of our being, so long as we are occupied in stopping it with mud. So the saint is our evidence, and other men, of course, for the glimpses of sanctity that are in them.

Said or Sung, p. 139

203

St John the Evangelist

27 December

The pagan would wish to show that his divine hero was supremely original, but St John's testimony is that his divine Saviour is utterly derivative. This is the point which the Jews in the Gospel dialogue cannot understand. They accuse Jesus of claiming to be someone, of seeking his own glory, of bearing testimony to himself. His reply is that of himself he is nothing and claims nothing; that is just how he differs from us men. We seek glory for ourselves, and we seek it from one another. Jesus has nothing to do with anything of the sort. What he does do is to speak the words his Father sent him to speak and perform the acts his Father puts into his hands. He cannot forbear to claim that these are the words, the acts of God, for then he would be failing to do his errand. He must demand submission to the messenger of God in the name of God, even though he happens himself to be that messenger. But 'messenger' is inadequate; a messenger merely reports a set of words entrusted to him, but what is entrusted to Jesus is the very life and love of God, to be lived in the world and made to shine and to save. If I give a written message to the college messenger he can say, 'All right, sir,' and put it in his pocket. If I give him a verbal message he can say, 'All right, sir,' and put it in his head. It is all right, because when his pocket is crammed with notes and his head with messages, he has still plenty of room for being himself. But if I say to him, 'Don't take a message, just go and be me,' it isn't all right any more. He must reply, 'No, I am afraid I can't do that, sir; I am not you, I am myself, sir.' Sons in this world can no more be their fathers than messengers can be their employers; but the divine Son can say, 'He that hath seen me hath seen the Father.'

The evidence, then, that Jesus was God-from-God and God-with-God, was that a life had come into the world which gave back to God the picture of his own face, and the love of his own heart. And the second evidence was the power of it. By union with this life men received a share in something not human at all, an eternal divine sonship.

Said or Sung, p. 91

204

The Holy Innocents

28 December

I was a shown the other day a distressing passage in Dr Leslie Rouse's autobiography. It transcribes an old letter, almost too painful to be read, from a relative of his, a simple countrywoman, who has lost a young child. She complains of the unendurable agony imposed on her by the ancestral belief that whatever happens is the direct will of God Almighty. It is intolerable to see the perfect little body deprived of life; it is double torment to have to think that God has done it to you. Be rid of the monstrous hypothesis, deny God, and you can reach some kind of peace.

One cannot disagree with the conclusion: only one can point out that the unhappy mother has stood religion on its head. We do not begin with the assurance that everything is under the hand of almighty Providence. We begin from a world touched with glories and shot through with agonies, and we call upon the God of glory to deliver us from the wicked fiend. The bereaved mother who has no God to implore is in no better case, far from it, than one who believes in him. Their miseries are equal; but one calls on a saviour, the other grins and bears it. Religion begins with the God of Salvation; and we do not ask him to save us from himself, we ask him to save us from our enemy and his. Whether we personify the forces of evil or not is a side-issue. If we do personify them as Satan, we are at least clear that we do not identify them with God. As with disasters, so with temptations; they are not the direct inflictions of a divine pastoral strategy, twisting our tails for the good of our souls. God does not need to invent temptations for us; the waywardness of our desire, the low standards of our neighbours, the cross-accidents inevitable in a world of creatures freely moving, will provide us enough trials and to spare. We cry to the God of Salvation to rescue us from the mischief which would else frustrate our worthy purposes.

A Celebration of Faith, pp. 181, 182

INDEX OF SUBJECTS

This index supplements the framework of ASB Sunday themes used throughout the book.

———